Christ Church Cathedral, reredos. St. Louis Public Library.

St. Louis:
Historic Churches & Synagogues

by Mary M. Stiritz

with Cynthia Hill Longwisch
and Carolyn Hewes Toft

Bibliography by
  Jean E. Meeh Gosebrink

Financial assistance provided by

The Missouri Department of Natural Resources, Division of State Parks,
  Historic Preservation Program.

The Donald and Ruth V. Malvern Foundation.

The St. Louis Convention & Visitors Commission.

Acknowledgments

Landmarks Association began a four-year architectural survey of historic St. Louis churches and synagogues in 1990. Funded by a series of matching grants from the Missouri Department of Natural Resources, the citywide survey was conducted by Mary M. Stiritz and Cynthia Hill Longwisch who visited and photographed over 350 sites. Summer interns helped out along the way, especially Nancy Kaiser. Discussions in 1994 about a publication led to the decision to join forces with the St. Louis Public Library. The Library had received a grant from the St. Louis Convention & Tourism Commission to help produce a booklet on St. Louis historic churches and synagogues similar to its guides to German-American and African-American sites. Once again, a matching grant from the Missouri Department of Natural Resources provided the funding essential to enlarge the project.

During the year of research and production, major collections of historic photographs and drawings were inventoried. Special thanks for assistance in this effort are due Jean Gosebrink at the St. Louis Public Library, Duane Sneddeker at the Missouri Historical Society, Charles Brown at Mercantile Library, and Martin Towey from the St. Louis Archdiocese. Other historic images came to us on loan from various church archives. Landmarks' survey photographs, the major source for contemporary views, were carefully augmented by the work of Robert C. Pettus - an architectural photographer with an unerring eye. Invaluable consultation about the citywide survey was received from Esley Hamilton. Others who provided insight include Melanie Fathman, Carolyn Herkstroeter, and David Simmons. A special debt of gratitude is owed Dorothy Baumann, who set up a computer program that allowed the analysis of more than 350 sites.

Deliberations about just which representative examples should be featured in this book were difficult. Consideration was given to geographical balance, chronological inclusiveness, ethnic diversity, denominational variety, and architectural significance. Sometimes the choice was made to select a relatively unknown site in preference to one previously published; other decisions were based on the availability of accurate research sources. The result is an attempt to introduce the reader to one medley rather than the full score of St. Louis religious treasures. Future editions will add new themes.

ISBN: 0-937322-10-5

Looking east from Lafayette and Fourteenth Streets, c. 1923. St. John Nepomuk is in the center. Landmarks collection.

Table of Contents

Introduction

There are many ways to look at ecclesiastical buildings: method of construction, materials, ornament, stained glass, etc. Style and floor plan are two common approaches which help us understand the building within a specific cultural context and time period. The rich variety of styles chosen for religious buildings in St. Louis generally followed the national trends which were fashionable in any given period. The city is fortunate to have excellent examples of these styles. The following overview of styles and floor plans is intended to introduce the reader to some of the major design themes in the building history of St. Louis churches and synagogues.

CLASSICAL REVIVAL

By the mid-1840s, blocks closest to the early riverfront settlement displayed a clustering of Classical-style churches, the first national style adopted by St. Louis denominations. However, the Old Cathedral (#1), the city's first monumental church building, would soon become the sole survivor in the central corridor.

By the 1850s, commerce and the "Almighty Dollar" had been enthroned as the new "divinity that reigns above the church sites," according to a *Globe-Democrat* reporter in 1884 who criticized the levelling of early shrines for business blocks and reflected on the "willingness with which growing cities part with their landmarks."

The life span of many Protestant churches at their original sites rarely exceeded twenty-five or thirty years. Typical of the westward migration pattern, the Unitarian Church of the Messiah erected its first church in 1837, a Classical Doric-style building at Fourth and Pine Streets. Subsequent moves took the congregation first to Ninth and Olive in 1850; then to Garrison and Locust in 1880; next to Union and Enright (#51) in 1907; and finally to Waterman near Kingshighway in 1917. By contrast, inner city Catholic churches generally remained in the same location where they continued to serve new immigrant groups who settled in the old neighborhoods. Daughter churches of the original parishes, however, followed the expanding city into new subdivisions.

First Unitarian Church or Unitarian Church of the Messiah, northwest corner Fourth and Pine Streets, c. 1842. (Razed)
Architect unknown. J. C. Wild: watercolor on paper. Missouri Historical Society.

Pilgrim Congregational Church on "Piety Hill," southeast corner Ewing and Washington Avenue, 1890. (Razed) Designed in 1867 by Henry Isaacs, St. Louis. Photo: E. Boehl. St. Louis Public Library.

GOTHIC REVIVAL

The Gothic Revival style made its first St. Louis appearance in 1839 when the congregation from Christ Episcopal Church completed its second building (demolished) at Chestnut and Fifth (Broadway) Streets. At that time the Classical style still dominated St. Louis church design. However, as new residential sectors opened in the next western tier of urban settlement, the Gothic Revival style steadily gained acceptance. Blocks around Lucas Place boasted some of the city's finest Gothic Revival churches of the 1850s and 1860s. Two churches remain: Christ Episcopal (#6) and Centenary Methodist (#15). Farther west, post-Civil War Gothic Revival churches anchored all the church corners on "Piety Hill," as the Stoddard Addition was called.

Variants of the Gothic style continued to be built in St. Louis into the mid-twentieth century. Overall, Gothic was the style most often chosen by a majority of congregations. Some denominations, such as Lutherans and Episcopalians, adopted Gothic to the near exclusion of other styles. The reasons for the style's great popularity and longevity can be traced to nineteenth-century England. Intense study of pre-Reformation medieval England led architects and scholars to conclude that the Golden Age of Christian society occurred during the period when the Gothic cathedrals were built. The belief that Gothic was synonymous with the "true Christian style" was sustained with only minor dissent until the modern period. American Gothic Revival churches were also indebted to nineteenth-century England for terminology which subdivided the style into phases known as Early English, Decorated, and Perpendicular.

First Methodist Episcopal Church, South, northwest corner Eighth and Washington Avenue (razed). Designed c. 1853 by George I. Barnett, St. Louis. John Hogan, Thoughts about St. Louis, 1854. St. Louis Public Library.

ROMANESQUE REVIVAL

Concurrent with the construction of Gothic-style churches were houses of worship which exhibited Early Romanesque Revival, the first of the round-arched Romanesque styles to gain favor nationally. The Early Romanesque Revival was also known by alternate names, including Byzantine, Norman, Lombard, and *Rundbogenstil* in Germany – the source for the American version of the style. Two of St. Louis' earliest examples, Union Presbyterian Church and First Methodist, South, were both designed by George I. Barnett in the early 1850s. The churches were located in what is now downtown St. Louis.

The Early Romanesque's simple design conventions and restrained ornament were well-suited to St. Louis' tradition of brick construction. The relatively inexpensive brick Romanesque church became quite popular with newly formed congregations of various denominations throughout the city. Numerous Catholic parishes adopted Romanesque for their first or second church buildings, as did, for example, St. Bridget (#5) and St. Boniface (#8). In the second half of the nineteenth century, the Evangelical church, now the United Church of Christ, commonly chose Early Romanesque. Examples include Carondelet German Evangelical (#17) and St. James Evangelical German (#26).

Although permutations of Early Romanesque never completely died out in St. Louis, the style was revitalized in the mid-1890s. Architect Albert B. Groves drew up plans for two 1890s Protestant churches (#37 - Aubert Place Congregational and Curby Presbyterian) which employed the tall bell tower or campanile associated with the northern Italian "Lombard" subtype of Early Romanesque. In the twentieth century, the Romanesque became most closely identified with Catholic church design in St. Louis.

RICHARDSONIAN ROMANESQUE

Richardsonian Romanesque, a later variant of the Romanesque style, was introduced into St. Louis design traditions in the mid-1880s.

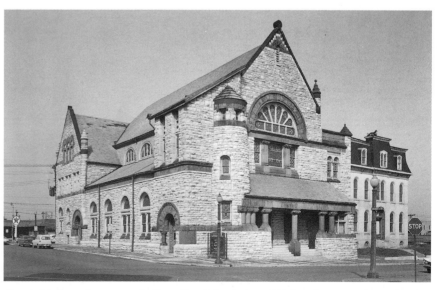

Temple Israel, northeast corner Leffingwell and Pine Streets, 1960, (razed). Designed in 1888 by Grable & Weber, St. Louis. Photo: Landmarks collection.

The style was named after the nationally prominent architect Henry Hobson Richardson from Boston (1838-86) whose 1872 design for Trinity Episcopal Church (Boston) was widely imitated. In contrast to the brick tradition of the Early Romanesque style, Richardson preferred the more rugged effect achieved by the use of rock-faced stone as a building material.

Mainline Protestant congregations relocating after the 1870s to more westward neighborhoods around or beyond Grand Avenue typically chose Richardsonian Romanesque. First Congregational Church (#22), one of the first St. Louis churches designed in the Richardsonian manner, was built on Grandel Square a block west of Grand

oldest congregation of that denomination in the city) erected an impressive stone Richardsonian Romanesque church. The building was the first church constructed by and for an African-American congregation. During the 1890s, Richardsonian Romanesque rivaled the popularity of Gothic in St. Louis churches. In 1899, Second Presbyterian Church (#43) began construction of the city's closest quotation of Richardson's Trinity Church (see page 21).

TWENTIETH-CENTURY CLASSICAL

Because of the association of the Classical style with "pagan" religious temples of ancient Greece and Rome, the Classical styles never achieved broad acceptance in St. Louis church

St. Paul's African Methodist Episcopal Church, southwest corner Lawton and Leffingwell, 1890, (razed). Architect unknown. Missouri Historical Society.

Avenue. An early notable exception to the Protestant domination of Romanesque, Temple Israel (a prominent Jewish reform group) adopted the style for their first synagogue, an 1887 design by Weber & Groves (St. Louis). In 1890, St. Paul's African Methodist Episcopal Church (the

St. John's Methodist Church in "Holy Corners," northwest corner Washington and North Kingshighway. **Photo: Robert C. Pettus, 1974.** *Landmarks Association.*

design after the Neoclassical/Greek Revival period of the 1840s and 1850s. A few noteworthy exceptions are found in the turn-of-the-century Classical-style churches that form the Holy Corners group on Kingshighway (#45-48). Later, the patriotic identification of the Colonial Revival style as the "true American style" with roots in the country's colonial heritage produced a few churches in that variant of classicism. Scruggs Methodist Church (#69), built in 1929, was the first Colonial Revival design in St. Louis.

The Church of Christ, Scientist exhibited the strongest classical presence of any one denomination in St. Louis. Local Christian Science buildings reflected a national pattern found in the denomination's buildings across the country. With the endorsement of Mary

TWENTIETH-CENTURY GOTHIC

The last great flowering of the Gothic Revival in St. Louis during the 1920s and 1930s was given impetus by the Boston architect

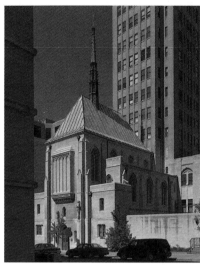

Chapel. St. Louis University Hospital (Firmin Desloges), 1325 South Grand. Designed in 1933 by Ralph Adams Cram, Boston. **Photo: Robert C. Pettus, 1995.** *Landmarks Association.*

Second Church of Christ, Scientist, 5807 Murdoch, 1955. Designed in 1940 by Carl Schloeman, Chicago. Photo: Mercantile Library.

Baker Eddy (the Boston founder of the Christian Science church), Chicago architect Solon S. Beman (a convert to the faith) became the leading designer for the Christian Scientists. Beman found an affinity between the Classical style and the rational theology of Christian Science belief. The architect's designs set a precedent for Christian Science churches in St. Louis that continued to exert influence as late as 1940 when the former Second Church of Christ, Scientist (now Roosevelt Bank) was erected.

Ralph Adams Cram (1863-1942), whose interpretation of Gothic exercised wide national influence up to World War II. Like earlier nineteenth-century English architects, the scholarly Cram found inspiration in the Christian Middle Ages. Cram expounded his medievalism in extensive writings, and, of local interest, in the inaugural lecture of a series sponsored by the American Institute of Architects, which took place in St. Louis in 1934. The series honored Cram's friend and fellow medievalist Henry Adams, the author of *Mont Saint Michel and Chartres*, a book published by the American Institute of Architects.

While visiting St. Louis, Cram saw for the first time his only design in the city: the 1933 chapel in then Firmin Desloges Hospital, which he asserted was "as pure fourteenth-century Gothic as I could make it." In a *Star-Times* interview captioned "Architect Cram Flays 'Hellish' Modern Designs," Cram declared that the modern style was unsuitable for churches and should be confined to buildings which had no link with the past, such as movie theaters and department stores. Most St. Louis architects shared Cram's medieval bias. Their churches show influence of his precepts and designs, as, for example, Memorial Presbyterian Church (#62).

The majority of new churches constructed in St. Louis in the 1940s and 1950s continued to employ historic revival styles. Many of these designs, however, were simplified and streamlined under the influence of modernism. St. Mark's Episcopal Church (#75), completed in 1939 to designs of Nagel & Dunn (St. Louis), received local acclaim as the city's first bona fide modern style church. A major leap into modernism, Resurrection Catholic Church (#77) by Murphy & Mackey (St. Louis) experimented with new architectural forms and progressive liturgical art.

STYLE AND ETHNICITY

St. Louis' impressive number of ethnic houses of worship illustrates diverse cultural developments in the nineteenth and early twentieth centuries. By 1880, the city boasted one of the richest ethnic mixes in the United States. First- and second-generation foreign groups accounted for at least two-thirds of the population. Stylistic imagery of religious buildings became an important vehicle for establishing ethnic identity in the city's diverse neighborhoods.

Congregations turned to familiar Old World monuments to evoke images of the homeland. The styles of the churches, along with liturgical art, strengthened both internal and external perceptions of ethnic unity and distinctiveness.

Shaare Emeth Synagogue, northeast corner 17th and Pine Streets, 1875, (razed). Designed in 1869 by Thomas W. Brady, St. Louis. Centenary Methodist (extant) tower visible to the right rear. David B. Gould, St. Louis Illustrated, 1872. St. Louis Public Library.

Neighborhood churches and temples became the most visible collective symbols of the foreign communities.

German and Irish Catholics were the principal immigrant church builders in St. Louis. German parishes, assisted by German-trained architects, constructed churches which recalled the great cathedrals in Germany [St. Liborius (#29), Most Holy Trinity (#39), and St. Francis de Sales (#55)]. English or Irish churches tended to inspire the designs of local Irish churches such as St. Francis Xavier Catholic Church (#24) and St. James the Greater (#67). Italian Catholics of St. Ambrose parish (#61) looked to northern Italy for an ethnic model. When Shaare Emeth (the first Reform congregation in the city) built in 1869, they followed a nineteenth-century Jewish tradition of using "oriental" Moorish forms and ornament as a way to distinguish the synagogue from Christian churches. The Moorish style was believed to be evocative of the Jewish people's Middle Eastern origins. In St. Stanislaus Kostka (#31), the Byzantine style elicited a

St. Liborius German Catholic Church, 1835 North 18th Street, 1955. Church designed in 1889 by William Schickel, New York City. Tower designed by Joseph Conradi, St. Louis, added in 1907, but removed in 1965. Photo: Buzz Taylor. Landmarks collection.

spirit of Polish nationalism. Exotic Byzantine domes and towers of the Eastern Orthodox traditions continued to punctuate the city's skyline in Holy Trinity Serbian Church (1928), St. Michael's Russian Church (#68), and St. Thomas Romanian Church (1959).

BASIC FLOOR PLAN TYPES

A floor plan usually reveals the type of worship for which a church was intended. Thus, a church designed for a denomination which emphasizes liturgy and ritual requires the formal architectural setting provided in a plan that focuses on the chancel and altar. Such churches tend to be rectangular, longitudinally oriented, and are longer and narrower than churches designed for non-ritualistic congregations where preaching or reading is a primary element of worship. The latter church plans focus on the pulpit and the arrangement of pews around it. These churches generally utilize a more compact square or polygonal plan shape found in designs known as central or auditorium plans.

Longitudinal plan: St. Leo's Roman Catholic Church, northwest corner 23rd and Mullanphy Streets, 1978, (razed). Photo: Landmarks collection.

LONGITUDINAL/BASILICAN PLAN

This elongated plan takes the shape of a rectangle. The altar usually occupies one end of the rectangle (sometimes in a space known as the chancel) with the entrance narthex or vestibule commonly placed within a tower at the other end. The central space between the entrance and the far end of the rectangle is called the nave.

If the longitudinal plan is intersected by transepts (short "arms" that project beyond the outside walls of the nave and aisles) to form a cross shape, that design is known as a cruciform plan.

Basilican plan: Most Holy Trinity, 3519 North 14th Street, c. 1900. Landmarks collection.

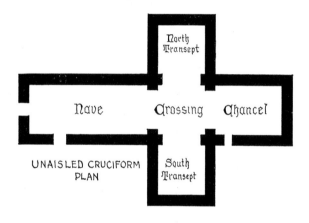

Cruciform plan: F. R. Webber, *The Small Church: How to Build and Furnish It*. (Cleveland, Ohio: J. H. Jansen, 1939) 36.

clerestory windows, so named because these windows "clear" and rise above the rooftops of the side aisles. As with other longitudinal churches, the basilica is entered through a narthex or vestibule and terminates with an outward projection called the apse at the altar-end of the church. The name and design of the plan derive from the ancient Roman basilica, a secular building used by the Romans for courts of law and commerce. During the fourth century when Christianity became the state religion of the Roman Empire, the basilican plan was adapted to religious purposes. Denominations which frequently employ the longitudinal/basilican plan include Roman Catholic and Episcopal, although it is found in other groups as well.

HALL-CHURCH

A basilica, a type of longitudinal church, also follows the rectangular plan, but the basilican plan is distinguished by the introduction of rows of columns which separate the broad nave from narrower flanking side aisles. The ceilings of the side aisles are lower than the ceiling of the center nave. The upper walls of the nave are pierced with

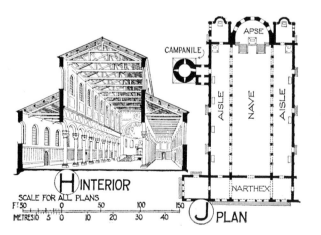

Basilican plan: Sir Banister Fletcher, *A History of Architecture*, 17th ed. (New York: Charles Scribner's Sons, 1967) 264.

Although a member of the basilican plan group, the hall-church differs from it in the treatment of the interior space. In a hall-church, the nave and side aisles rise to ceilings of approximately the same height.

A single roof usually covers both nave and aisles. (Because a basilican church nave is taller than the side aisles, separate roofs are necessary.) The hall-church is closely associated with German Catholic church design in St. Louis. The design was used extensively in North German medieval churches; nineteenth-century Germany recognized the hall-church as an important German development invested with nationalistic associations.

The major building period for hall-churches in St. Louis began in the last quarter of the

Hall-church plan. Private collection.

Hall-church plan: SS. Peter & Paul, 1919 South 7th Street. **Photo: Robert C. Pettus, 1973.** *Landmarks Association.*

nineteenth century and ended in 1910. During that time, eleven of the twenty-one German Catholic parishes had either planned or built hall-churches. This period of church building coincided with an era in which ethnic consciousness reached unprecedented heights. Before the completion of SS. Peter & Paul's hall-church in 1875 (#18), little specifically "German" was discernible in the design of the German parish churches. As the German Catholic community grew in size and strength, a desire for German identity emerged. Internal diocesan polemics between the Irish-dominated hierarchy and German priests over the unequal status of foreign-language parishes also heightened ethnic consciousness.

Three churches designed in the 1890s by Louis Wessbecher, a German-born and -trained architect who practiced in St. Louis, illustrate the way in which design may be used to express ethnic identity: Polish Catholic St. Stanislaus Kostka (#31) employs a domical centralized plan; Bethlehem Lutheran, an auditorium plan; and German Catholic St. Augustine's, a hall-church. German parishes which built churches after World War I corroborate other evidence of the disappearance of German ethnic expression because of anti-German sentiment. The churches no longer follow the hall-church design but are based instead on English medieval models with low side aisles and large clerestory windows.

CENTRALIZED/AUDITORIUM

The square or polygonal shape of this plan type serves to unify the congregation and the center of worship by drawing them together in closer proximity than is offered by the longitudinal plan. A centralized plan church that is covered by a large dome usually signifies a congregation which traces its heritage to Eastern Europe and the Eastern Orthodox (Byzantine) Church (e.g., St. Michael's Russian Orthodox, #68). It may also indicate a congregation that associates its cultural roots with Middle Eastern architectural traditions as with some Jewish congregations (e.g., United Hebrew, #64).

Central plan: Sacred Heart Catholic Church, 2830 North 25th Street, 1986. Photo: Landmarks Association, Cynthia Hill Longwisch.

The auditorium plan, a centralized type developed by nineteenth-century American Protestant churches, created optimum conditions for hearing and viewing. Theater architecture became the model for church auditorium design because theaters offered well-developed solutions to the problems of acoustics, sightlines, and performance space. Church architects borrowed and adapted standard amphitheater features. These features included curved pews arranged in a fan shape on a floor inclined toward the front, and a raised "stage" or platform for the pulpit which sometimes was banked by additional tiers for the choir and organ. St. Louis' numerous examples include Washington & Compton Avenue Presbyterian Church (#19), Compton Hill Congregational (#34), and Lafayette Park Methodist (#44).

AKRON PLAN

By its strictest definition, the term Akron plan refers to a design for a separate Sunday school building which was erected in 1867 as an adjunct to the First Methodist Church in Akron, Ohio. This Sunday school plan appeared at a time when religious education for children of middle-class Protestant families was increasing in importance and in degree of specialization. The Ohio building's plan offered a practical solution to the Sunday school requirements for both assembly and compartmentalized space. It featured a semi-

Auditorium plan: Pilgrim Congregational Church, southeast corner Ewing and Washington Avenue, c. 1890, (razed). Photo: E. Boehl. St. Louis Public Library.

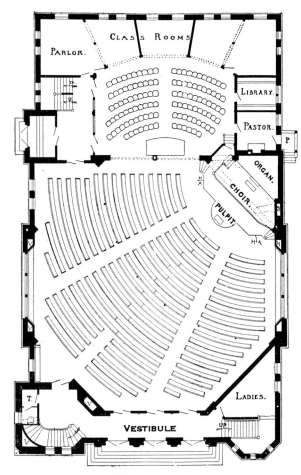

FLOOR PLAN

Auditorium-Akron plan: F. E. Kidder, <u>Churches and Chapels</u>. (New York: William T. Comstock, 1906) plate xxiv.

circular auditorium/assembly room ringed with separate classrooms. One of St. Louis' earliest examples of this arrangement of school rooms is Cook Methodist Church (#23) designed in 1884.

In its broader usage, the Akron plan may refer only to the design feature of recessible wall partitions which open adjacent lecture rooms or halls to the main church auditorium. This feature was well-suited to square auditorium plan churches and usually is found in combination with that plan. The recessible or folding doors were widely adopted to provide additional seating space for overflow church crowds. Variants of the Akron plan received extensive coverage in the architectural press which published church plans as well as advertisements for recessible doors. The plan flourished in St. Louis from the 1870s to about

1910 when its popularity declined. The former Hyde Park Congregational Church (now Faith Temple Pentecostal) at Bremen and Blair Streets retains one of the most fully developed Auditorium/Akron plans in St. Louis. It was designed in 1894 by Minneapolis architect Warren H. Hayes who specialized in this plan type. All three floors in the church exhibit features of the plan. Another good example is found at the Aubert Place Congregational Church (#37) in Fountain Park.

CRITERIA FOR SELECTION

All of the churches and synagogues illustrated in this book are located within the present corporate boundaries of the city of St. Louis. The book does not include religious architecture in St. Louis County. Generally, architectural significance was the primary guiding principle for selecting churches and synagogues. In some instances, the social and cultural significance of various congregations also contributed to the selection process. The seventy-seven houses of worship chosen for description, however, by no means represent all that are worthy of recognition. Many other fine examples of religious architecture could not be included in this edition because of limitations of space and time. A number of the featured churches in this book have been formally acknowledged at one or more levels of designation. These are indicated by sets of initials following a church's current name:

NHL: National Historic Landmark

NHS: National Historic Site

NR: National Register of Historic Places - individual listing

NRD: National Register of Historic Places District - listed within a district

CL: City Landmark - individual listing

CHD: City Historic District - listed within a local district

Second Presbyterian Church. **Photo: Robert C. Pettus, 1975.** *Landmarks Association.*

Old Cathedral, March 1940. Landmarks collection.

Old Cathedral, November 1940. St. Louis Public Library.

Old Cathedral, 1892.
Photo: E. Boehl. St.
Louis Public Library.

1. "Old Cathedral" NHS, CL
Basilica of St. Louis, the King of France
209 Walnut Street (at Third Street)
1831: Morton & Laveille, St. Louis

The Old Cathedral is the fourth Catholic church constructed on the city block set aside for that purpose in 1764 by St. Louis founders Pierre Laclede Liguest and Auguste Chouteau. Built at what was then the exorbitant cost of $63,361, the church (measuring 136 x 84 feet) is one of the finest erected in the young republic of the United States up to the time of the 1830s. Its Joliet, Illinois, limestone facade features a 40-foot-wide portico supported by four Doric columns; a crowning pediment inscribed with gilded Hebrew characters expresses the ineffable name of God as worshipped by both

Christians and Jews. Originally, six large stone candelabra (now removed) embellished the parapet wall. The neoclassical interior is articulated with two rows of five Doric columns made of brick with stucco finish.

Bishop Joseph Rosati, the first to hold that title in the new diocese of the Upper Louisiana Territory, selected architects George Morton (a native of Edinburgh, Scotland) and Joseph Laveille (born in Pennsylvania) to design the cathedral. The firm had gained recognition from their designs of St. Louis' First Episcopal Church (1826), the first courthouse, and early buildings at Jefferson Barracks.

The large construction deficit ($58,000) left by Rosati "retarded the progress of religion in this diocese by twenty years at least," according to Bishop Peter Richard Kenrick, Rosati's successor. To reduce this debt, Kenrick leased vacant land and constructed commercial rental property in the cathedral's city block; proceeds benefited the church. After the Civil War, however, Kenrick moved from the crowded cathedral site and adopted St. John the Apostle's Church (#7) farther west as his cathedral and residence.

Gradually, multi-storied buildings surrounded the Old Cathedral, overwhelming its once impressive stature. The only historic structure not razed for the Jefferson National Expansion Memorial, the church (now an icon) was renovated in 1963 by architects Murphy & Mackey (St. Louis), who added a new rectory at the rear.

St. Mary of Victories, c. 1900. St. Louis Public Library.

2. St. Mary of Victories Roman Catholic Church
St. Stephen's Hungarian Parish NR, CL
744 South Third Street (at Gratiot Street)
1843; 1859: George I. Barnett, St. Louis

By the early 1840s, the large number of German Catholics who had emigrated to St. Louis increased the demand for German priests and a church exclusively for German use. Under the leadership of Irish-born Bishop Peter Richard Kenrick, St. Mary of Victories became the first of St. Louis' many German-language national parishes. On June 25, 1843, the cornerstone of the new church was laid; but only the nave (74 x 44 feet) could be completed by 1844 due to the large diocesan debt incurred during construction of the Old Cathedral. The transept-apse (69 x 69 feet) and belfry, added in 1859-60 following the original cruciform plan, brought total costs to $13,000.

Constructed of red brick, the church has a monumental facade articulated with engaged brick piers supporting a wood-trimmed pediment. The open, three-bay nave features a painting of "The Coronation of the Virgin" on the flat ceiling. Tall, round-arch stained glass windows installed in 1844 exhibit geometric patterns in muted colors. St. Mary's church is one of the few remaining buildings designed by St. Louis' preeminent nineteenth-century architect, English-born George I. Barnett (1815-98). Trained in London, Barnett arrived in St. Louis in 1839 and began a long, distinguished career that included important residential, commercial, and ecclesiastical commissions.

Once the focal point of a dense German immigrant neighborhood, the parish was already in decline by the late nineteenth century as residential buildings gave way to industrial uses. Nearby, demolition in 1940 for the Jefferson National Expansion Memorial, followed ten years later by the construction of an elevated highway within yards of St. Mary's doorsteps, accelerated this decline. In 1957, the church was turned over to a Hungarian congregation whose dedicated members breathed new life into St. Mary's through a series of fund-raising projects which included concerts and Hungarian suppers.

St. Vincent de Paul. **Photo: Robert C. Pettus, 1975.** *Landmarks Association.*

3. St. Vincent de Paul Roman Catholic Church   NRD, CL
1417 S. Ninth Street (at Park Avenue)
1844: George I. Barnett, St. Louis

Bishop Rosati named this church after the patron saint of his own order. Rosati placed the fledgling parish under the pastoral care of the Vincentian Fathers in 1838 and they are still there today. In contrast to St. Mary of Victories (#2), the German national parish located a few blocks away, St. Vincent's was intended to serve both English- and foreign-speaking Catholics in the new Soulard Additions. This status attracted a cosmopolitan group of parishioners including Germans, Irish, descendants of the founding French gentry, and members of the free "colored aristocracy."

The cornerstone of the red brick church was laid on St. Patrick's Day, 1844; consecration followed on November 5, 1845. The cruciform building designed by George I. Barnett measured 150 x 60 feet with a transept of 80 feet.

Construction costs reached $30,000, more than twice that of St. Mary's (#2). A few years after completion of the main body, the parish added a new facade, vestibule, and tower. The interior exhibits a fine Classical colonnade that divides the space into nave and side aisles. The Pickel Co. of St. Louis installed new marble altars circa 1888. In preparation for the 1895 Golden Jubilee, St. Vincent's commissioned Professor Jacob P. Hoegen to execute wall and ceiling paintings and to design art glass windows. The four large paintings depicting St. Vincent de Paul were based on French steel engravings.

The parish once boasted an impressive complex of Classical Revival buildings, including Benjamin A. Soulard's 1837 mansion. Adapted as the diocesan seminary and priests' house, the building was razed in 1952 along with other parish property for construction of Interstate 55. The three-story rectory of 1857, shown to the left of the church in the above photo, has also been demolished. The 1859

Boys' School (later Vincentian Press Building) to the right is still standing and holds the distinction of being the oldest public or private school building in the city.

SS. Cyril & Methodius, 1995. Photo: Landmarks Association, Cynthia Hill Longwisch.

4. SS. Cyril & Methodius Polish National Catholic Church NRD
North Presbyterian Church
2005 N. Eleventh Street (at Chambers Street)
1857: Eugene L. Greenleaf, St. Louis

The former North Presbyterian Church is one of the city's oldest surviving examples of Early Romanesque Revival style, a style characterized by decorative brick corbeling on plain brick walls pierced by round-arched windows. A colony from First Presbyterian Church (#27), the congregation organized in 1845 in the newly platted town of North St. Louis, which included middle-class Anglo-American merchants, industrialists, and professionals. By the 1890s, the character of the neighborhood was in transition as industry encroached and new immigrant groups arrived.

North Presbyterian sold the building in 1908 and moved west, eventually locating in a

1917 Gothic Revival building (designed by Albert Meyer) on the northeast corner of St. Louis Avenue and Warne Street. The new owners, members of SS. Cyril & Methodius Polish National Catholic Church, belonged to a denomination founded in 1896 in Scranton, Pennsylvania. Formed by dissident Polish Roman Catholics from St. Stanislaus (#31) and St. Casimir's, SS. Cyril & Methodius was one of the first parishes in what was destined to become the largest American schism of the Roman Catholic Church. Early in their history, Polish National Catholics introduced progressive reforms in the areas of ownership of church land, church governance (they gave a voting voice to women), and noncompulsory celibacy for priests. Today, SS. Cyril & Methodius serves a parish of some fifty families, many of whom are third generation members. Architect and builder Eugene Greenleaf (1815-81; active in St. Louis 1847-79) remains best known for his later designs of pavilions, gazebos, and well houses in Henry Shaw's Tower Grove Park.

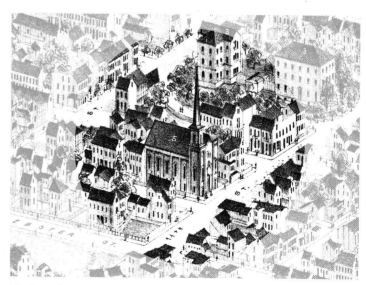

North Presbyterian Church, Compton & Dry: Pictorial St. Louis, 1875. Plate 45.

St. Bridget of Erin, 1991. Photo: Landmarks Association, Cynthia Hill Longwisch.

5. St. Bridget of Erin Roman Catholic Church

1100 N. Jefferson Avenue (at Carr Street)
1859: John F. Mitchell, St. Louis

On August 7, 1859, the cornerstone was laid for this Early Romanesque Revival building of red brick trimmed with white stone. The building measures 75 x 135 feet. The interior features a nave colonnade of slender clustered columns supporting a lattice-like open-timbered ceiling. Born in Ohio, architect John Mitchell trained in the St. Louis office of an uncle, Stuart Mathews, before becoming a prominent church architect. Other Mitchell designs include Immaculate Conception (1853, Seventh and Chestnut) and St. Nicholas (1867, Nineteenth and Lucas), both demolished.

St. Bridget, founded in 1853 in a small brick church (since razed) adjacent to the present church, was destined to become the mother church for Irish Catholics. Although its original parish boundaries included promi-nent families living west of Jefferson Avenue in the fashionable Stoddard Addition, St. Bridget became closely identified with Kerry Patch -- a working-class Irish neighborhood that grew up to the east. An Irish-born priest was assigned to the first little building. Another Irish-born

St. Bridget of Erin, c. 1940. Mercantile Library.

priest, Father William Walsh, paid the debt on that building, built two schools, a rectory, and laid the groundwork to complete the present church steeples.

Described in 1928 as but a shadow of its former self, St. Bridget was reduced to about seventy-five parishioners by 1948. In the early 1950s, construction of its new neighbor, the nearly 3,000-unit Pruitt-Igoe housing project, infused new, if temporary, life into the church. Father Walsh's rectory (the "Irish castle") and his brick schools were demolished for replace-ment buildings (Murphy & Mackey, St. Louis) hailed by the press as more in keeping with the new neighborhood. Total demolition of the thirty-three 11-story buildings in the Pruitt-Igoe complex began in 1975. This left 70 acres un-touched by new construction until the ground breaking in 1994 for a new public school north of St. Bridget. The church has about 230 parish-ioners today.

*Christ Church
Cathedral, c. 1920.
St. Louis Public
Library.*

*Christ Church Cathedral, reredos assembly, c. 1912.
St. Louis Public Library.*

6. Christ Church Cathedral NHL, CL
Christ Episcopal Church
*320 N. Thirteenth Street (at Locust Street)
1859: Leopold Eidlitz, New York
1910: Kivas Tully, St. Louis*

This English Decorated Gothic-style church was designed in 1859 by Prague-born New York architect Leopold Eidlitz (1823-1908), one of America's most prominent nineteenth-century designers. Considered the architect's masterpiece, Christ Church Cathedral is the oldest of thirteen extant churches built by the Episcopal Church in St. Louis between 1859 and 1938. The cornerstone was laid on April 22, 1860, but financial problems and the onset of the Civil War delayed completion. In 1867, when services were first held, it still lacked a tower and porch which were finally added in 1910-12 by St. Louis architect Kivas Tully. Tully closely followed Eidlitz' design. He also designed a new 18-foot-high bishop's chair, a Carrara marble altar, and a 35-foot reredos (screen behind the altar) incorporating fifty-three figures carved in England by sculptor Harry Hems using stone from Caen, France.

In 1929, interior walls were partially lined with Guastovino tiles. Except for the open-timbered ceiling, the church is all stone construction including tracery in the windows. The earlier portion employs Illinois sandstone; the tower and porch are Indiana limestone. The majority of the stained glass belongs to the original construction period and is the work of Owen Doremus of Montclair, New Jersey. Windows in the west bay of the north aisle were executed by Tiffany of New York in 1917. The six-story Bishop Tuttle Memorial Building (erected 1927-28 from designs by Jamieson & Spearl, St. Louis) replaced the Schuyler Memorial House of 1892 (by Shepley, Rutan & Coolidge of Boston) and the sandstone Bofinger Chapel of 1893 (by James B. Legg of St. Louis). The chapel was moved to abut the south transept. In 1969, Burks & Landberg (St. Louis) reworked the nave to accommodate secular concerts and plays.

painted by Russian artist Adolphus J. Oloff.

The eighth Catholic parish in the city, the church was affiliated with the Archbasilica of St. John Lateran in Rome and could thus hold ordination and consecration services. In 1876, St. John's became the Pro-Cathedral – the residence and administrative center for Archbishop Kenrick and his staff. Kenrick left the Old Cathedral engulfed by the grime and noise of the mercantile city; yet within two generations, factories, budget hotels, and saloons surrounded St. John's as well. All family members of the parish had moved out by the 1930s, and the church ministered exclusively to transients and travelers from nearby Union Station.

In 1949, the federal government passed legislation creating the far-reaching urban renewal program. The Plaza Square area, 54 blocks including St. John's, was chosen by the city to be the first local project. Massive demo-

7. St. John the Apostle and Evangelist Roman Catholic Church CL

15 Plaza Square (at N. Sixteenth and Chestnut Streets)
1859: Patrick Walsh, St. Louis

At its inception in 1847, St. John's parish encompassed an area of farms and forest west of the growing city. The cornerstone of the present church was laid May 1, 1859; dedication followed November 4, 1860. Meanwhile, Irish-born Patrick Walsh, the original architect of the church, had resigned because of structural problems discovered during initial construction. Thomas Mitchell succeeded him and supervised the work following Walsh's design. The red brick Lombard Romanesque Revival church features a barrel-vaulted nave and, over the main altar, a copy of Raphael's "Transfiguration"

St. John the Apostle, c. 1900. Mercantile Library.

St. Boniface, c. 1900. Archdiocesan Archives.

lition began in 1953. Construction of the six 13-story Plaza Square Apartments by Harris Armstrong with Hellmuth, Obata & Kassabaum (St. Louis) got under way a few years later. The Archdiocese renovated St. John's as part of the project, selecting Murphy & Mackey (St. Louis) as architects. According to a *St. Louis Post-Dispatch* article of the time, the architects, after surveying St. John's "mixture" of styles, "decided to work for an Italian Renaissance effect with contemporary touches." Alterations included the lengthening of side windows and the removal of tower windows and moldings. The nave received new windows by Unique Art Glass.

8. St. Boniface Roman Catholic Church
7622 Michigan Avenue (at Schirmer Street)
1860: Thomas W. Brady, St. Louis

Named in honor of St. Boniface, the Apostle of Germany, this church was built to serve German Catholics living in Carondelet, which was a separate city until its annexation by St. Louis in 1870. On May 5, 1860, the cornerstone was laid for the red brick Early Romanesque Revival church. The building measures 126 x 56 feet. Twin towers, each 100 feet high, date to 1868 (south) and 1890 (north). The original nave, featuring an open-timbered ceiling with ornamental woodwork, was replaced circa 1880 by the present plaster vaulted ceiling hung under the trusses. Paintings executed in 1882 by Charles F. Krueger enrich the apse and side walls. Stained glass by the Tirolean Glass Works of Innsbruck was installed in 1894. Architect-woodcarver John H. Dreisoerner created new side altars, statues, and a communion rail in 1909. In 1921, Ludwig & Dreisoerner designed a new parish house; a school followed in 1948.

Little is known about Irish-born architect Thomas Brady, who also received commissions for Annunciation Catholic Church (1859) and Shaare Emeth Synagogue (1869), (see page 14), both since razed. The 1870 census reported that Brady was 38 years old, married, held real estate valued at $15,000, and had a personal estate of $10,000. He submitted plans, as did Patrick Walsh (see #7), for the Governor's Mansion (Jefferson City) in 1871, but lost out to George I. Barnett.

9. True Life United Pentecostal   NRD
Zion German Evangelical Lutheran Church
1426 Warren Street (at Blair Avenue)
1860: Henry Brueggemann, St. Louis

As the oldest extant Lutheran house of worship in St. Louis, Zion's two-story, red brick building combined both church and school. This was a typical multi-purpose use practiced by young congregations throughout the nineteenth and early twentieth centuries. Laying of the cornerstone for the Classical Revival building took place on July 2, 1860; it reached completion in December of that year at a cost of $8,474, which included a sixteen-pipe organ. One of Zion's members, carpenter Henry Brueggemann, handled construction, receiving

Zion German Evangelical Lutheran, c. 1890. Private collection.

lated area of north St. Louis. Within two years this school evolved into the fourth offshoot of Trinity Lutheran (#41), the mother church in Soulard. Despite financial hardships during the Civil War, Zion built a two-story brick school in 1868 that still stands at the rear of the church. In 1895, the congregation moved into a new stone Gothic Revival church (#36) located at North Twenty-first and Benton Streets. Zion sold the 1860 building in 1909. The church was occupied during the early 1920s by the Greeley Memorial Presbyterian congregation, followed by the Zion Church of the Nazarene. A rug cleaner tenanted the building briefly during the Depression. Since 1937, the church has been home to a series of Pentecostal congregations.

assistance from a building committee of fellow members who represented the building trades: a brickmaker, a lumber dealer, and another carpenter.

The congregation started in 1858 as a school of Immanuel Lutheran (#65) in a densely popu-

10. Carondelet Markham Memorial Presbyterian Church
Carondelet Presbyterian Church
6120 Michigan Avenue (at Bowen Street)
1863; 1895: Architects unknown

Carondelet Markham Memorial Presbyterian, 1991. Photo: Landmarks Association, Cynthia Hill Longwisch.

The oldest Protestant church building in the former independent city of Carondelet (annexed in 1870), the 1863 brick church is one of only a few Civil War-era churches remaining in the city. Beginning in a log building at another location two blocks north, the congregation erected a frame church on the present site in 1849. Founders of Carondelet Presbyterian included Henry T. Blow, a Carondelet industrialist and U.S. Congressman who gave land for a parsonage. His daughter, Susan Blow, famous for her public school kindergarten, played a prominent role in the church's Sunday school.

Construction of the new brick church came to a halt with the onset of the Civil War. After roofing foundation walls, the congregation worshipped in the basement until 1865 when the rest of the building was paid for by the women of the church with money raised from "prayer, tears and strawberries." The completed design displays affinities with Early Romanesque Revival. The adjoining stone Richardsonian Romanesque Revival church erected in 1896 contains a handsome 500-seat auditorium with an open-timbered ceiling. This feature resembles truss designs by architect John G. Cairns for other 1890s-era churches (#27, #30, #33). In 1958, the congregation merged with Markham Memorial Presbyterian Church, which moved here from Menard and Julia Streets in the LaSalle Park neighborhood.

Architect Ted Wofford outlining plans for the renovation of the Shrine of St. Joseph, 1977. Photo: Artega.

11. The Shrine of St. Joseph NR, CL
St. Joseph's Roman Catholic Church
1220 N. Eleventh Street
1865: Thomas Waryng Walsh (Walsh & Smith), St. Louis
1880: Adolphus Druiding, St. Louis

Little if anything remains of the Neoclassical church built on this site in 1844. From the first, the German-speaking congregation received pastoral care from Jesuit priests who assisted architect Walsh in planning the existing 1865-66 nave, an addition that enlarged the church's dimensions to 185 x 85 feet. Influence of seventeenth-century Italian Baroque models can be seen in a richly embellished interior and also in the twin-towered facade. The latter was already planned in 1866 when a St. Louis journalist compared St. Joseph's exterior to Roman churches and the interior specifically to seventeenth-century St. Annunziata in Genoa.

Paintings from the 1865 building program, including colossal apse figures of the Virgin and four saints, were executed by French-born artist Leon Pomerade, known for his river "panoramas" and for frescoes in numerous St. Louis public buildings. The main altarpiece, carved by Bueschers of Chicago in 1867, reportedly followed the design of the Altar of St. Ignatius in the Jesuit Gesu Church in Rome. It is dedicated to St. Joseph in thanksgiving for his divine intercession during St. Louis' 1866 cholera epidemic. One of the parish Jesuit priests created the elaborate pulpit; three windows by Franz Mayer of Munich were installed in 1894.

The church is also noteworthy as the site of a miracle leading to the canonization in 1888 of Peter Claver (1581 - 1654), a Spanish Jesuit priest: in 1864 parishioner Ignatius Strecker miraculously recovered from myriad afflictions after kissing a relic of Peter Claver at St. Joseph's. St. Peter Claver's dedicated work among African slaves in South America gained official recognition in 1896 when he became the patron saint of all Catholic missionary work among blacks.

By the opening of the twentieth century, the

St. Joseph's, c. 1950. Landmarks collection.

neighborhood around St. Joseph's was becoming increasingly industrial and blighted. Only twenty families remained in the parish by 1944. Control of the church passed to the Archdiocese in 1965 and speculation about demolition began. Persistent rumors prompted Landmarks Association of St. Louis to engage local architect Ted Wofford in 1976 to study renovation costs. That report and the formation of the Friends of St. Joseph led to renovation of the church and the 1865 three-story brick rectory. This project provided a catalyst for the building of the Columbus Square neighborhood of townhouses and apartments.

Architect Thomas Waryng Walsh (1826-1890) was born in Kilkenny, Ireland, and trained in the Dublin office of Sir William Dean Butler. After working in Boston and New York, he began his St. Louis career around 1850. Walsh's designs include the first Lindell Hotel (1856), the Four Courts Building (1869), several public schools, banks, and the still-extant Bronson Hide Building (1856) in Laclede's Landing. During Walsh's 1860-73 partnership with James Smith, the firm designed St. John's Methodist Church (#12) and supervised the construction of St. Alphonsus Church (#13). St. Francis Xavier (College) Church (#24) was his last known ecclesiastical commission.

St. John's Methodist. Compton & Dry: Pictorial St. Louis, 1875. Plate 71.

12. Former St. Charles Borromeo Roman Catholic Church

St. John's Methodist Church, South
2901 Locust Street (at Ewing Avenue)
1867: Thomas Waryng Walsh, St. Louis

Although vacant and shorn of its Gothic pinnacles, finials, and spire, this church still retains much of the picturesque profile admired at the cornerstone-laying on June 27, 1867. A local newspaper identified the style as "Decorated English Gothic now so successfully carried out in England by Scott, Streets and others." St. John's, officially organized in 1868 after construction began, brought a Methodist presence to the fashionable new

neighborhood known as "Piety Hill." Centenary Methodist Church (#15) contributed to the building fund.

St. John's was described in 1882 as "one of the largest, wealthiest and most influential churches in the city." By the close of the nineteenth century, the congregation elected to move westward. A majority of members already lived in new residential areas as far west as the city limits. St. John's erected a new church (#45) in 1901 on Washington Avenue. In 1902, the old church was sold for $25,000 to St. Charles Borromeo's parish, which had recently been organized by Italian-born Father Caesar Spigardi (1859 - 1931). Spigardi was a dedicated immigrant church builder often regarded as the apostle of St. Louis Italian Catholics.

Prior to 1900, the Italian immigrant population in St. Louis was not sufficiently numerous to support a national church. Under Father Spigardi's leadership, three Italian parishes came to life between 1900 and 1903: Our Lady Help of Christians (10th and Cole, razed), St. Charles Borromeo, and St. Ambrose (#61). Spigardi oversaw all of these from his residence at St. Charles Borromeo. The Italian neighbor-

Former St. Charles Borromeo, 1990. Photo: Landmarks Association, Cynthia Hill Longwisch. Razed, August 1995.

hood around the church, composed largely of Sicilians and Neapolitans, gained notice for open-air processions in honor of the Virgin Mary. The interior of the church was extensively renovated in 1957. The building, now privately owned, has been closed since 1981.

13. St. Alphonsus Roman Catholic Church "Rock Church" CL

1118 N. Grand Avenue (at Cook Avenue)
1867: Reverend Louis Dold, St. Louis,
modified by Thomas Waryng Walsh, St. Louis
1893: Joseph Conradi (Schrader & Conradi),
St. Louis

Reportedly the first large stone church in the city, St. Alphonsus had already acquired its popular name, "Rock Church," in the nineteenth century. The building of white, rock-faced St. Louis limestone was erected by the Redemptorist Fathers (or Congregation of the Most Holy Redeemer), an order founded in the eighteenth century by St. Alphonsus Liguori, whose name the church bears. Built for Redemptorist missions and spiritual retreats, the church stood in the virtually unpopulated outskirts of the city at the time of the cornerstone laying on November 3, 1867. St. Alphonsus' status changed in 1881 to a parish church, which later became predominantly Irish.

Construction progressed slowly because of a shortage of funds, leading to the establishment in 1868 of an innovative Building Association. Members contributed 25 cents monthly. Upon dedication on August 4, 1872, the church still lacked its soaring stone steeples. They were completed in 1894 by architect-sculptor Joseph

Conradi. The ornate interior includes 1889 Gothic side altars and a high altar in marble by Peter Theis of New York City. The high altar features a center figure of St. Alphonsus. Conradi & Schrader (St. Louis) supplied a marble altar rail in 1890 and, in 1893, the "Our Lady's Shrine," which incorporated an image of the Virgin presented to the Redemptorists by Pope Pius IX in 1867. Early twentieth-century mosaics enrich the south transept wall where the altar stands. Large figural stained glass windows in the transept are among thirty-one in the church produced by Mayer of Munich. They cost $647 each. Installed just before the 1904 St. Louis World's Fair, the windows served

Our Lady of Perpetual Help Altar, 1931. Photo: W. C. Persons. Missouri Historical Society.

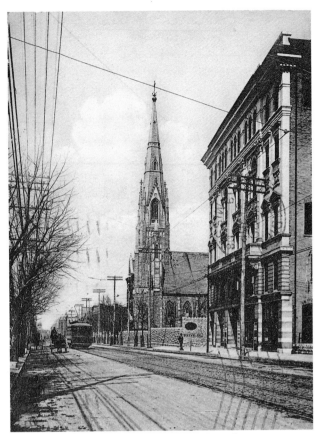

St. Alphonsus (Rock Church). Postcard looking north on Grand Avenue toward St. Alphonsus Church, 1908. St. Louis Public Library.

as a showcase for the German firm's booth at the Fair. One transept window is probably the 1870s glass work of Sutter & Bierworth (St. Louis).

Streetcar tracks laid on Grand Avenue in 1894 played an important role in the history of Rock Church. During the 1920s, "Our Lady's Shrine" began to attract thousands of area Catholics. In 1931, an average of 16,450 worshippers attended devotion each Tuesday, filling the church to many times beyond capacity. So many traveled to the service by streetcar that a "Novena" car was added to the line. Yet in 1928, diocesan historian Reverend John Rothensteiner wrote that the parish was in decline because of the "influx of Negroes and Jews." The prevalence of "Jim Crow" attitudes both in- and outside the church led to the 1941 opening within Rock Church's boundaries of St. Clement's parochial school and chapel for black residents. Segregation ended in 1947 thanks to the courageous leadership of Father

James Higgins who combined St. Clement's parishioners with those from St. Alphonsus and opened the church's doors to the black community. In more recent years, the Redemptorist ministry to black Catholics has brought a cultural renaissance and full attendance to St. Alphonsus. African-American gospel music "put the rock, that is, the rhythm — into the Rock" (*St. Louis Post-Dispatch*, July 6, 1990). New worship furnishings with African motifs designed by Jerzy Kenar (Chicago) symbolize a vital new spirit in St. Louis Catholicism. Renovations from 1990 by Murphy, Downey, Wofford & Richman (St. Louis) highlight elements of the interior space.

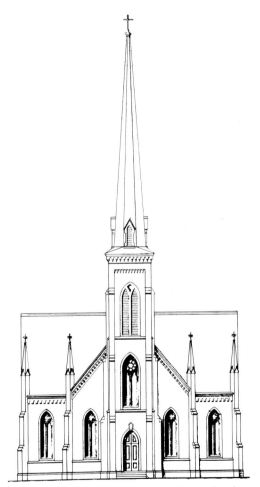

Drawing of Holy Cross Lutheran, c. 1867. Landmarks collection.

14. Holy Cross Lutheran Church

2640 Miami Street (at Ohio Avenue)
1867: Charles Griese (Griese & Weile),
Cleveland

The selection of Charles Griese as architect for Holy Cross Church can be traced to the recommendation of Reverend C. F. W. Walther, the official head of all St. Louis German Lutheran churches. Walther, the pastor of Trinity Lutheran (#41), directed Griese "to design a church in the form of a cross" following nineteenth-century Lutheran tradition. Because of budget contraints, only the four-bay nave and tower were completed by the time of the dedication on December 8, 1867. The arm and head of the cross (the transept-apse) were added in 1889 along with balconies. A close cousin of this red brick church stands in Cleveland, Ohio; the design was adapted in 1873 by the same architect for Trinity Lutheran there.

In 1896, a tornado tore off the original 160-foot steeple of Holy Cross; it was soon replaced, but by one less lofty. In 1905, the church received gifts of a marble replica of da Vinci's "Last Supper" and a painting of "Christ in Geth-semane." New art glass enriched the transept windows, while portrait windows of Martin Luther and Reverend Walther, dating to 1911, graced the nave. Other windows were replaced in 1926. The front of the church gained two additional entrances in 1908. A school on Ohio Street dating to 1914 is still in use.

In the nineteenth century, Holy Cross stood in a neighborhood stronghold of major Lutheran institutions: Concordia Seminary (removed to suburban Clayton in 1926), Lutheran Hospital, and Concordia Publishing House, both still close by but in new buildings. It began as a school organized in 1850 to serve

members living southwest of the mother church, Trinity Lutheran. In 1858, Reverend Walther officially organized the Holy Cross congregation as a subsidiary of his *Generalgemeinde*, an umbrella congregation composed of four district churches.

Detail: Holy Cross Lutheran, 1990. Photo: Landmarks Association, Mary M. Stiritz.

Holy Cross Lutheran, 1990. Photo: Landmarks Association, Cynthia Hill Longwisch.

Services were held in the chapel of Concordia Seminary until 1867 when the new church opened under the German name *Die Kirche zum Heiligen Kreuz* (The Church of the Holy Cross). After Walther's death in 1887, Holy Cross and other district churches became autonomous congregations.

15. Centenary United Methodist Church CL
Centenary Methodist Episcopal Church, South
55 Plaza Square (N. Sixteenth Street at Pine Street)
1868: Thomas Dixon, Baltimore, with Jerome B. Legg, St. Louis

The one hundredth anniversary of John Wesley's founding of Methodism was celebrated worldwide in 1839. This event provided the perfect occasion for the organization and naming of Centenary Church. The second Methodist church organized in St. Louis, Centenary built a Neoclassical house of worship in 1842 at the southwest corner of Pine and Broadway (George I. Barnett, architect). The building lot, purchased in 1840 for $10,500, had become prime commercial property by 1868 when its sale realized $142,000. This formed a healthy down-payment toward a new church to be built beyond the business district.

Constructed of North St. Louis limestone, the imposing structure features a towering 200-foot steeple and a facade design that architect

Centenary United Methodist, 1955. W. C. Runder Photo Co. Centenary Methodist Church.

Centenary United Methodist, 1990. Photo: Landmarks Association, Mary M. Stiritz.

Thomas Dixon later used again for Mt. Vernon Place Methodist in Baltimore. Centenary's 60 x 106-foot auditorium, with Gothic panelled galleries on three sides, remains a showcase of wood craftsmanship as exhibited in the largely black walnut ceiling, wainscoting, pews, pulpit, and chancel. A stone office building and parsonage, part of the original church design, face Pine Street.

An interesting side note is that at the laying of the cornerstone on May 10, 1869, church members placed an unusual but timely item in the ceremonial metal box: a telegram announcing the driving of the last spike for the Union Pacific Railroad at Ogden, Utah.

In 1900, when most downtown churches had moved west, Centenary made a long-term commitment to remain in the city. Extensive improvements at that time included new art glass windows. In 1903, membership numbered 1,642 and came from all over the city. Attendance peaked at 3,601 in 1930, but decline was inevitable as the neighborhood continued to change. Clearance for the Plaza Square

Apartments in the 1950s isolated Centenary. Today, the residents of those apartments provide the nucleus for a growing church that once again attracts members from throughout the region.

16. Jamison Memorial Christian Methodist Episcopal Church
Holy Communion Episcopal Church
609 Leffingwell Avenue (at Washington Boulevard)
1870; 1876: Henry G. Isaacs, St. Louis

Officially organized in 1869, Holy Communion Episcopal Church grew out of a mission Sunday School located nearby. The school and subsequent church stood in a 72-block subdivision known as Stoddard's Addition. Drawing affluent residents and their churches from older city sectors, the upscale tract gained the nickname "Piety Hill." Henry Isaacs, architect of the church, lived a few blocks away and served on the first vestry.

Built in two phases, the 1870 transept served as a chapel until enlarged by a 700-seat nave in 1876. The sound quality was so poor that the building was considered an "absolute acoustic failure." This defect purportedly was improved by stretching wires the length of the transept.

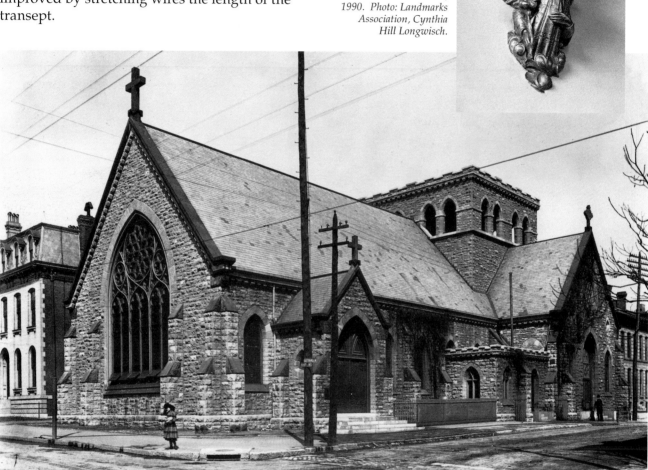

Detail: Jamison Memorial C. M. E., 1990. Photo: Landmarks Association, Cynthia Hill Longwisch.

Holy Communion Episcopal, 1894. Missouri Historical Society.

The rock-faced limestone walls of the structure are typical of the increased use of stone in post-Civil War churches following the opening of new quarries in Missouri and Illinois. The English parish church style is also representative of a new trend of the period. Noteworthy interior features include an open-timbered ceiling that springs from carved gilt angel corbels and vividly colored stained glass in floral designs. Pressed tin on the ceiling is a later addition. The original entrance through an east porch has been removed and replaced by two gabled doorways on the south (Washington Boulevard) facade.

As the neighborhood entered a period of transition, the church began to advertise its services on streetcars. This proved a successful if somewhat "unchurchly" device for attracting new worshippers. Through extensive social services such as a playground, a daily kindergarten, and a free clinic, the early twentieth-century parish responded to the new needs of an area increasingly characterized by boarding houses and commerce. Finally, in 1945, long after other neighborhood churches had moved west, Holy Communion sold the building. The new owner was Jamison Memorial C. M. E. Church, a black congregation organized in 1917, which came to Washington Avenue from 2800 Clark Street.

Architect Henry Isaacs (1835-95) was born in Philadelphia and raised in New York City. He trained in the New York office of Richard Upjohn. His St. Louis career began in 1855 with George I. Barnett. Most of Isaacs' best-known designs have been demolished, including some large commercial buildings and Pilgrim Congregational's church on "Piety Hill." The Mercantile Library Building downtown remains, but it is sheathed.

at the national level in 1934. This led, in 1939, to the Carondelet congregation's adoption of the name Evangelical and Reformed. In 1957, following the consolidation of the Congregational Christian Church with the Evangelical and Reformed Church, it was renamed United Church of Christ.

Two other nineteenth-century German Protestant churches still stand in Carondelet: St. Trinity Lutheran (1872) at Vermont and Koeln and Carondelet German Methodist (1897) on Virginia at Koeln.

17. Carondelet United Church of Christ
Carondelet German Evangelical Church
7423 Michigan Avenue (at Koeln Avenue)
1871; 1902: Architect unknown

Through the efforts of German missionary pastors in the area, the German Evangelical Church Association of the West became an organized body in 1840. "North America" replaced "West" as the denomination expanded. While sharing religious views held by the Evangelical church in Germany (an 1817 union of Reformed and Lutheran Churches), the North American group remained autonomous. The *Deutsche Evangelische Gemeinde in Süd St. Louis* (German Evangelical Congregation of South St. Louis), organized in 1869, served German-speaking settlers in Carondelet.

The church's simple rectangular plan with a central tower entry in a gable-front became a familiar design for St. Louis Evangelicals. Early Romanesque Revival-style round arches and decorative brickwork on plain masonry walls are also characteristic of the denomination's nineteenth-century churches. The nave (90 x 140 feet), with paneled wood ceiling, reached completion in 1871 at a cost of $4,570. In 1902, the congregation spent $36,000 to add a chancel, a choir room, and a sacristy. Ten new figural stained glass windows from the Emil Frei Co. studio (St. Louis) were installed in 1944. A hall from 1926 adjoins the rear of the church.

Denominational name changes took place

Carondelet United Church of Christ, 1945. Photo: Donald Dates. Missouri Historical Society.

SS. Peter & Paul, 1890. Photo: E. Boehl.
Missouri Historical Society.

18. SS. Peter & Paul Roman Catholic Church   NRD, CL , CHD

1919 S. Seventh Boulevard (at Allen Avenue)
1873: Franz Georg Himpler, New York

SS. Peter & Paul was organized in 1849 to serve a rapidly growing immigrant neighborhood. It became the mother church of south side German Catholics. This is the third church building erected in the same city block purchased by the young parish in the early 1850s and gradually built by them into an impressive complex. Father Francis Goller (pastor 1858-1910), Westphalian-born and -educated, deserves credit as the motivating force behind construction of this monumental stone church. He was impressed by German-trained architect Franz Georg Himpler's 1870 design for a German Catholic church in Detroit, and invited the architect to St. Louis in 1872.

When the cornerstone was laid, German-language newspaper coverage described SS. Peter & Paul as a German Gothic hall-church design following fourteenth-century models. Its close adherence to medieval construction methods was cited as an unusual feature. Many fine examples of German craftsmanship can be found in the liturgical art, including the stained glass windows imported from Innsbruck, Austria, and the stations of the cross (1895) in oil on canvas executed by the Beuron School of Art (founded in 1894 by Benedictine architect and sculptor Desiderius Lenz at Beuron, Germany). In 1890, the stone tower was completed following Himpler's design at a cost of $33,000. The interior of the church was renovated in 1984. A circular seating arrangement replaced the original pews designed for a crowd of 3,000.

Father Goller's prominent national role as an advocate for parochial school education is reflected in the school buildings he erected at SS. Peter & Paul. An 1889 rectory designed by

SS. Peter & Paul, 1890. Photo: E. Boehl.
Missouri Historical Society.

German-trained Ernst Janssen and the 1905 recreation building (Goller Hall) date from his tenure. Today, many of the turn-of-the-century parish buildings have been converted to social service uses. The growing parish of 285 families supports a hospitality house for families with patients in St. Louis hospitals. Residents of a men's shelter located in the church basement help other Soulard inhabitants pick up litter left by crowds at popular neighborhood bars or events such as the local Mardi Gras celebration.

Lafayette Park Presbyterian after 1896 tornado. St. Louis Public Library.

19. Washington Tabernacle Baptist Church CL
Washington & Compton Avenue Presbyterian Church
3200 Washington Boulevard (at Compton Avenue)
1877: John H. Maurice, St. Louis

Designed by John H. Maurice and constructed of St. Louis limestone trimmed with sandstone, this building closely resembles the Lafayette Park Presbyterian Church (1878). The latter was also designed by Maurice, who was a member of that congregation. Columns of polished Maine granite embellish the main entrance on Compton. Large rose windows on side elevations and an 18-foot triangular window on the principal facade afford a well-lighted interior. Roof construction featured a "heavy Howe truss" system, described at the time as a structural innovation.

The church plan also presents new architectural trends of the period. The nearly square 84 x 88 -foot main auditorium on the second floor is a departure from traditional rectangular plans. The intent was to improve acoustics and increase the visibility of the pulpit by eliminating columns. Curved pews arranged amphitheater-style on an inclined floor are encircled by a balcony. Modified Akron-plan Sunday school rooms and a lecture room, originally connected by folding doors, are located under the auditorium on the ground floor. A fire in the late 1940s severely damaged the interior.

Washington Tabernacle Baptist, 1995. Photo: Landmarks Association, Cynthia Hill Longwisch.

The Washington & Compton Presbyterians began their history as a breakaway group of conservatives who, together with pastor James Brookes, withdrew from Second Presbyterian Church on Broadway in 1864 and moved into a new building on Walnut Street, which had just been completed for Second Church. Walnut Street Presbyterians prospered. In 1877, members paid $15,000 for a 140 x 152-foot lot two miles west of downtown at Washington and Compton. Ground was broken for the new church on the fourth of July that year. A colony withdrew in 1878 to form a church in Lafayette Square, closer to their homes, but work continued at the Washington and Compton site. The lecture room was occupied on May 1, 1879. The first services in the completed sanctuary were not held until December 1880.

Members once again voted to move west in the 1920s, naming the new church Memorial Presbyterian (#62). Tabernacle Baptist, organized in 1902, purchased the building at Washington and Compton. Over the years Tabernacle has been the home of many local black leaders. Dr. Martin Luther King, Jr. selected Tabernacle as the site for a major civil rights rally in May 1963, just before the March on Washington.

20. Abyssinian Missionary Baptist Church
Second German Swedenborgian Church
2126 St. Louis Avenue (at Rauschenbach Avenue)
1883: Architect unknown

Swedenborgians, or the New Jerusalem Society, were first organized in St. Louis in 1842. Largely an English-speaking congregation, the church established a German society in 1854 for the growing number of immigrants who followed the teachings of Emmanuel Swedenborg (1688-1772), the Swedish scientist, philosopher, and theologian. The building, erected in 1859 by the First German Society, still stands at North Fourteenth and Howard Streets. It was modified in 1878 and 1885 by a secular singing group, the *Nord St. Louis Bundeschor* (North St. Louis Choral Society).

The Second German Church of the New Jerusalem was organized in 1879. Four years later they constructed this red brick building in the heart of a prosperous north side German neighborhood. A star and the date 1883 appear at the peak of the facade gable. On the side elevations, black brick outlines pointed arches and creates horizontal beading. The interior has been remodeled.

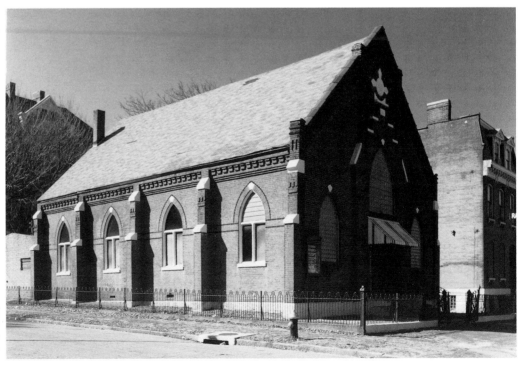

Abyssinian Missionary Baptist, 1995. Photo: Landmarks Association, Cynthia Hill Longwisch.

The Swedenborgians occupied the church until 1930. The Chiesa Diddio Christian Italian Pentecostal Church held services there briefly. In 1937, the Italian Christian Congregational Church moved in and remained there until 1956. From 1960 to 1972, the building was home to the Church of God Prophecy; it has been the Abyssinian Missionary Baptist Church since 1973.

21. Memorial Church of God in Christ
Garrison Avenue Baptist Church
620 Spring Avenue
1884: Architect unknown

to a new, larger, stone church at Delmar and Pendleton (#30).

The new owners in 1892 were the First Society of the New Jerusalem (or Swedenborgians). Organized in 1842, the group waxed and waned over the years, then reorganized anew in 1877. The congregation moved to 620 Spring Avenue from its 1878 church (razed) on Lucas near Ewing. In the mid-1930s, this church with 120 members was the only New Jerusalem congregation in St. Louis and one of about fifty in the country. The Swedenborgians owned the Spring Avenue building until 1956 when title passed to the Church of God in Christ, the present owners.

Memorial Church of God in Christ, 1990. Photo: Landmarks Association, Cynthia Hill Longwisch.

The Garrison Avenue Baptist congregation, an offspring of Third Baptist Church, built its first small church in 1877 on Garrison near Morgan (now Delmar). Only two years later, that building was moved west to the corner of Morgan and Compton where the Baptists worshipped until 1884 when this Gothic Revival building was completed. Only eight years later the congregation reorganized as Delmar Baptist, sold the building, and moved

The interior of Memorial Church of God in Christ features a simple wood-paneled ceiling with pointed-arched ribs marking bay divisions. Vertical sliding glass doors (a partial Akron plan) partition the auditorium from auxiliary rooms in the balcony. Facade windows in the church display a Decorated English Gothic tracery pattern in the form of a circle inset with a six-pointed star.

First Congregational Church, c. 1915. Mercantile Library.

22. Grandel Square Theatre NRD
First Congregational Church
3610 Grandel Square
1884: Hurd & Rice, Boston

The First Congregational Society, the first church of that denomination in St. Louis, came into being in 1852 when a majority of Third Presbyterian Church members voted to become Congregationalists. Presbyterians and Congregationalists, sharing similar doctrine, had combined forces and money earlier in the nineteenth century to establish missionary churches in the Missouri Territory. Backed by Congregationalist dollars, Presbyterians founded several churches here in St. Louis before the Congregationalists established churches in their own name.

By the late 1870s, First Church's downtown building at Tenth and Locust (an 1853 George I. Barnett design) was too distant from where most members lived, prompting the purchase of the present Grandel Square lot and the construction of a temporary frame chapel. Plans for a new church designed by the Boston firm Hurd & Rice apparently came about through the influence of church member E. C. Rice, who was the brother of architect Lewis Rice (1839-1909), an engineer with the St. Louis waterworks in 1867-71. One of the first St. Louis churches to adopt the Romanesque Revival style of H. H. Richardson (Boston), the Grandel Square building recalls in particular the tower of Richardson's Brattle Square Congregational Church in Boston. (The St. Louis church tower now lacks its red tile pyramidal roof.) Firms involved in construction (listed at the dedication in April 1885) were: ornamental and stained glass, Union Sign Works Co.; stone masonry, H. S. Hopkins Co.; cut stone, William Clark; carpenter work, Melburn & Rich; frescoing, R. D. Bowman; wood mantels, A. A. Prawl; tiling & marble works, T. J. Foy; pews, Haynes, Spencer & Co. of Richmond, Indiana; pulpit and other furniture, L. & L. Niedringhaus; and terra cotta (frieze on the tower), H. A. Lewis, Boston.

First Congregational remained in the Midtown church for nearly thirty years. In 1915, they moved into a new chapel on Wydown Boulevard in St. Louis County. The old church received a new lease on life in 1991 with the help of an NEA Challenge Grant. At a cost of $4.5 million, it was recycled as the Grandel Square Theatre, the new home of the St. Louis Black Repertory Company in the Grand Center arts district.

Scruggs Memorial. **Photo: Robert C. Pettus, 1995.** *Landmarks Association.*

23. Scruggs Memorial Christian Methodist Episcopal Church
Cook Avenue Methodist Episcopal, South
3680 Cook Avenue (at Spring Avenue)
1884: Thomas B. Annan, St. Louis

The high value that Methodists placed on the role of the Sunday school is evident in the design of this church which features one of the earliest well-developed examples of an Akron plan remaining in the city. This plan type first gained recognition in a Sunday school designed

Scruggs Memorial. **Photo: Robert C. Pettus, 1995.** *Landmarks Association.*

for First Methodist Church in Akron, Ohio. Like Scruggs' school unit, the Akron church featured a semi-circular communal assembly-lecture room ringed with individual class-rooms. Architect Thomas B. Annan modified the Akron example (which had the school in a separate building) by connecting Scruggs' school to the main church auditorium through vertically sliding wood doors. This movable partition wall could be raised to provide addi-tional seating for overflow church attendance.

The school at Scruggs is richly articulated. The large assembly room culminates in a dramatic open-timber ceiling supported by ornamental cast-iron columns (by Christopher & Simpson, St. Louis). Classrooms feature decorative etched glass transom windows. The

main church auditorium also displays a hand-some open-truss ceiling and vivid stained glass in floral designs. One window includes a painted glass portrait of Richard M. Scruggs, founder of Scruggs-Vandervoort-Barney, a department store. Encaustic vestibule tile by T. J. Foy (St. Louis) is also noteworthy. Borrow-ing from theater designs that improve acoustics and sight lines, the auditorium employs curved pew seating on a floor sloping toward the pulpit.

Built of St. Louis limestone with Indiana limestone trim, Cook Methodist Church ap-peared to one writer in 1885 to be a "happy blending of early English style of pointed architecture and the Lombardic." Several prominent St. Louis businessmen who did not belong to the church contributed substantially to the building fund – notably Samuel Cupples and Robert Brookings, partners in the Cupples Woodenware Company. Cupples served both as a Trustee and a member of the Building Committee for Cook Methodist Church.

Architect Thomas B. Annan (1839 - 1904), a leading layman of the Southern Methodist Church, later designed Mt. Auburn Methodist Church (1891, razed) and the former Methodist Orphan's Home (1895) at 4385 Maryland Avenue in the Central West End. Annan is perhaps best known for his 1890 design for Samuel Cupples' sumptuous residence on West Pine, a project that purportedly cost more than five times the expenditure for Cook Methodist.

In 1872, a member of St. John's Methodist Church (#45), then at Locust and Ewing, established a Sunday school in the West End not far from the site of this church. St. John's subsequently sponsored the school; its success led to the organization of a church in 1877. Construction of the new stone church in 1884-85 became possible through a $35,000 gift (half the total cost) from St. John's member Richard M. Scruggs.

Scruggs had served as superintendent of the Sunday school since 1877; upon completion of the new church, he transferred his membership from St. John's to Cook Methodist Church. A noted philanthropist, Scruggs reportedly remarked, "They say I am foolish to give away so much, but wait until they see my will." True to his word, the dedicated churchman left Methodists a substantial sum, including $10,000 earmarked for the Cook Avenue church. A few years after his death in 1904, the congregation adopted their benefactor's name. In 1925, church ownership passed to the "Colored Methodist Episcopal Church" (after 1954, Christian Methodist Episcopal).

24. St. Francis Xavier Roman Catholic Church "College Church"   NRD, CL
3628 Lindell Boulevard (at Grand Boulevard)
1883: Thomas Waryng Walsh, St. Louis

Acting as anchors for a major intersection of Midtown, "College Church" (dedicated to St. Francis Xavier) and Dubourg Hall (1888) were the first buildings erected on the St. Louis University campus after the move from its original downtown location at Ninth and Lucas. Construction began in 1883 and the cornerstone was laid June 8, 1884, but work continued over many years. The tower was

St. Frances Xavier (College Church), c. 1930. Photo: W. C. Persons. Mercantile Library.

St. Frances Xavier (College Church), c. 1930. Missouri Historical Society.

finally completed in 1915. Designed by Irish-born Thomas Walsh with modifications by Henry W. Switzer of Chicago, the church was closely patterned after E. W. Pugin's nineteenth-century cathedral of St. Colman in Cobh, Ireland.

The lofty interior features English fan vaulting of wood and plaster. Granite columns support a brick Gothic arcade surmounted by a triforium arcade. Designed by the ateliers of Magry Bros. and Snickers (Rotterdam, Holland) and dedicated in 1899, the main altar conformed with the transitional English Gothic architecture of the church. The architectural

component of the altar came from the Pickel Marble Co. (St. Louis), and the statuary came from Carrara, Italy. Side aisles terminate with the Blessed Virgin and St. Joseph altarpieces, which were executed in Carrara marble by German sculptor Joseph Sibbel (1856 - 1907). Apse windows installed in 1929 (patterned after Chartres Cathedral) are the work of Emil Frei, Jr., who also designed the nave and rose windows installed 1936-38. Alterations in 1990 by Kurt Landberg (St. Louis) placed a central altar platform between the north and south transepts and introduced a new baptismal area.

Anzeigen der St. Peter und Pauls-Gemeinde.

STATIONS of the CROSS

ECCLESIASTICAL WORK
OF THE
HIGHEST ORDER

Wm. KLOER
· CHURCH-DECORATOR ·
916-18 ALLEN AVE · St. LOUIS Mo.

ALTAR
PIECES
AND HISTORICAL
PAINTINGS

PAINTING & GILDING
of STATUES AND
ALTARS

SCENERIES
for STAGES

William Kloer advertisement, 1900. Private collection.

St. Agatha. **Photo: Robert C. Pettus, 1974.** *Landmarks Association.*

25. St. Agatha Roman Catholic Church CHD

3239 S. Ninth Street (at Utah Street)
1884; 1899: Adolphus Druiding,
St. Louis

Organized in 1871 as a German-language parish for immigrants living in the neighborhood around the Anheuser-Busch Brewery, the congregation began construction of this red brick church in 1884. The 145 x 64-foot nave was enlarged in 1899 with a transept, sanctuary, and sacristy.   German-trained Adolphus Druiding had also drawn up plans for St. Agatha's first church of 1871-72, a two-story combination church and school. Its front-gabled facade trimmed with corbeled brickwork was retained in the second church. St. Louisan Joseph Stauder served as contractor for the 1884-99 church and as architect for additional buildings: a parish convent built in 1892, a priest's house erected in 1896, and a school built in 1909; together these form the existing ensemble.

Stauder's subcontractors included two south side firms: Dierkes & Hoogstret, who provided the brickwork (1884), and stone masonry by Erbs & Rieth. Inside, late nineteenth-century liturgical furnishings include a high altar dedicated to St. Agatha by Conrad Schmid (Milwaukee); side altars by Lansbeck & Macke of Louisville; stations of the cross by Ludwig Glaetzle of Munich; a Carrara marble baptismal font by F. X. Speh; and statues by Max Schneiderhahn and by A. T. Kaletta. George Hoffman constructed the clock in the tower. In 1905, Emil Frei Glass Co. (St. Louis) installed fourteen new windows. The church vestibule was refurbished circa 1920 in tile and marble. At the same time, a new Pieta shrine by Henry Dreisoerner was installed. Church decorator William Kloer frescoed the church in both 1899 and 1920.

26. St. James Community Center

St. James German Evangelical Church
1507 E. College Avenue (at Blair Avenue)
1887: August Beinke, St. Louis

Distinctive art glass windows embellish a simple vaulted nave of the *Deutsche Evangelische St. Jacobi Kirche*, as St. James was called by its German congregation. The church was formally organized in 1886. Prior to that, Eden Evangelical Seminary offered

intermittent services to the north St. Louis community once known as Lowell. A central tower along with the round-arched motif found in corbel tables and openings was a design

St. James, 1990. Photo: Landmarks Association, Cynthia Hill Longwisch.

Detail: St. James, 1990. Photo: Landmarks Association, Mary M. Stiritz.

convention favored by many nineteenth-century Evangelical churches. Architect August Beinke's vigorous Late Victorian interpretation of the *Rundbogenstil* (the German counterpart of Romanesque Revival) received notice in the architectural press of the time. The parish closed in 1984.

Born and raised in the German community of Washington, Missouri, August Beinke (c. 1846 - 1901) began his St. Louis career as a carpenter. Around 1873, he opened an architectural office downtown. During the early 1890s he practiced with John L. Wees. Beinke drew up plans for two other extant St. Louis churches: Union Methodist (1880) at Garrison Avenue and Samuel Shepard Drive, and German Zion Methodist (1897) in Carondelet.

27. Shiloh Church of God
First Presbyterian Church
4100 Washington Boulevard (at Sarah Avenue)
1888: John G. Cairns, St. Louis

This congregation, the cradle of St. Louis Presbyterianism, came to life in 1817 through the missionary efforts of Protestant pioneer Reverend Salmon Giddings (1782 - 1828). Giddings was sent to Missouri territory by an east coast alliance of Congregational and Presbyterian churches. The first church (1825) built by the congregation stood on Fourth and Locust Streets. Three decades later the 700-member group relocated to prestigious Lucas Place in a $100,000 Gothic church designed by Oliver Hart. Within a generation, however, encroaching commerce precipitated another move, this time to what was considered the far west at Sarah Street and Washington Boulevard.

The cornerstone was laid in 1888; the church was dedicated on October 27, 1889. Paying tribute to their past, the congregation interred Reverend Giddings' ashes in the new sanctuary and installed a bell from their first church in the tower. The design, executed in St. Louis limestone, followed the rugged, fortress-like Richardsonian Romanesque style that had gained popularity with Protestant denominations in the latter nineteenth century. The church's linear, rambling plan (accommodating the many spaces devoted to reception rooms and the Sunday school) was further enlarged about two years later with a Children's Chapel at the south end of the church. The architect's directions, as

Shiloh Church of God, 1988. Photo: Landmarks Association, Cynthia Hill Longwisch.

reported in 1889, focused on making the church "commodious and comfortable as well as artistically beautiful." Special features such as "cozy retreats" flanked the main auditorium and gave added comfort to the aged or infirm. Lighted by electricity, the structure boasted "all the modern improvements in every department."

The church proper and its auxiliary rooms all exhibit splendid wood furnishings. Open-truss ceilings in the Children's Chapel and the Akron-plan auditorium, arranged theater-style with curved pew seating on an inclined floor, are particularly fine. A large figural north window (reportedly designed by La Farge) was the gift of non-member William K. Bixby in memory of business associate William McMillan. Biblical inscriptions carved in stone form long horizontal lintels on the principal exterior walls. Tornado damage in 1927 removed a pyramidal spire.

Preparation for a fourth and final move began in 1923 with the purchase of a church site in University City. First Presbyterian completed the move in 1928. The building at Washington and Sarah was turned over to a new congregation, Giddings Presbyterian Church (later Giddings-Boyle).

St. Matthew's United Church of Christ, 1990. Photo: Landmarks Association, Cynthia Hill Longwisch.

28. St. Matthew's United Church of Christ

St. Matthew's German Evangelical Church
2613 Potomac Street (at Jefferson Avenue)
1888: Ernst C. Janssen, St. Louis

St. Matthew's was established in 1875 for members of St. Marcus Evangelical who lived too far away to attend that church (then at Third and Lafayette); the new congregation erected a brick church the same year at Cave and Seventh Streets near the Lemp Brewery. Changing conditions in the area dictated a move westward within a decade.

In 1886, St. Matthew's purchased the present lot, well situated near Benton Park in an established but still developing German neighborhood. Completed in 1889 at a cost of $33,432, the church welcomed the annual conference of the German Evangelical Synod of North America that spring when St. Matthew's was admitted into membership.

The Gothic design integrated an attached two-story gabled parsonage on Potomac. Although decorative brickwork recalls nineteenth-century Evangelical design conventions, the asymmetrical placement of the tower departed from the typical center tower plan. A brick school erected in 1894 on the north side of the church closed in 1910.

As was characteristic of German congregations, St. Matthew's hired a German-trained architect to design their house of worship. Born circa 1855 in Ohio of German parents, Ernst Janssen trained in the school of architecture at Karlsruhe, Germany where he won honors from the Grand Duke of Baden. Best known for his brewery designs in St. Louis and other American cities, and in Mexico, Janssen also drew up plans for the 1882 granite obelisk dedicated to Frederick Hecker in Benton Park, the rectory at SS. Peter & Paul (#18), and fourteen houses in Compton Heights, including the palatial Stockstrom House on Russell Boulevard.

29. St. Liborius Roman Catholic Church NR, CL

1835 N. Eighteenth Street
1889: William Schickel, New York
1907: Joseph Conradi, St. Louis

Since many of its members originally came from Paderborn, Germany, this parish became known as "Little Paderborn." They dedicated their first church in 1855 to St. Liborius, the patron saint of Paderborn, whose name was invoked by those suffering from gallstones. Early pastors were recruited from the Paderborn area. Construction of this church (the parish's second) began in 1888 to accommodate a congregation swelled by the influx of political and religious refugees from Bismarck's *Kulturkampf*.

St. Liborius' design came from the office of New York architect William Schickel (1850-1907), who was born and trained in Wiesbaden, Germany. Schickel, who began his American career with Richard Morris Hunt (New York), was well known for his designs of Catholic institutions in the East.

St. Liborius choir stall (sold in 1992 for $3,100), 1978. Photo: Landmarks Association, Janice Broderick.

St. Liborius' hall-plan church is constructed of red brick trimmed with white limestone. Following German models, the nave and side aisles (roofed as one) terminate in a trilobal east end formed by a polygonal apse and transept chapels. Inside, a five-bay nave arcade of slender columns carries quadripartite vaulting.

The parish maintained its cultural ties to Germany in the early twentieth century. In 1907, an 80-foot spire of filigree sandstone by Joseph Conradi (modeled after German spires such as Freiburg Cathedral's) was added, affirming the parish's strong

St. Liborius, 1978. Photo: Landmarks Association, Janice Broderick.

German heritage (see page 14). The spire was removed because of deterioration in 1965. New apse windows by Munich-born Emil Frei, installed circa 1907, portrayed events from the life of SS. Liborius and Boniface.

The church was closed in October 1991 and most of its furnishings were sold. Prior to that, the interior boasted seven marble altars carved by Conradi & Schrader (St. Louis), along with exceptional wood choir stalls, a pulpit, and the stations of the cross. An elaborate high altar given by the church's building contractors Bothe & Ratermann (parish members) still remains; it reportedly followed the design of an altar in the Church of the Franciscans in Duesseldorf. The parish ensemble includes an 1890 rectory by William Schickel and a 1905 convent of the Sisters of Notre Dame designed by parishioner Joseph Conradi (architect and sculptor).

Delmar Baptist, c. 1893. Photo: E. Boehl. Missouri Historical Society.

30. Galilee Baptist Church
Delmar Baptist Church
4300 Delmar Avenue (at Pendleton Avenue)
1891: John G. Cairns, St. Louis

The history of Delmar Baptist, originally organized as Garrison Avenue Baptist Church (an offshoot of Third Baptist, located on Clark near Fourteenth Street), illustrates an unusually rapid westward migration. The group erected its first church in 1877 on Garrison Avenue near Morgan (now Delmar), then moved that building in 1879 to the corner of Compton and Morgan where the congregation remained only five years. The year 1884 found them in their new stone Gothic church (#21) which still stands on Spring Avenue near Grandel Square. Within eight years, Garrison Baptist Church (by then renamed Delmar Baptist) relocated again, this time to the Romanesque Revival stone church at Delmar and Pendleton Avenues. Like many Protestant churches of the time, Delmar Baptist employed an Akron plan, integrating Sunday school rooms with the main auditorium through sliding doors. The centralized auditorium features a striking open-timbered mahogany ceiling (now painted white); the trusswork design resembles architect Cairns' ceilings in the 1888 First Presbyterian Church (#27) and 1892 Episcopal Church of the Redeemer (#33).

In 1914, Delmar Baptist sold the building to First Christian Church and eventually moved into their new stone church designed by William B. Ittner (St. Louis) at the southeast corner of Skinker and Washington Boulevards. First Christian sold the church in 1937 to the First Church of the Nazarene. The present congregation, Galilee Baptist, a black church founded in 1898, purchased the building in 1947 from the Nazarenes and installed new windows.

Born and educated in Scotland, John G. Cairns (c.1845-96) began practicing in St. Louis in the mid-1870s. In 1884, he married (and later divorced) a Presbyterian minister's daughter, Anna Sneed. Anna founded Forest Park University, a preparatory school for women that Cairns designed in 1890.

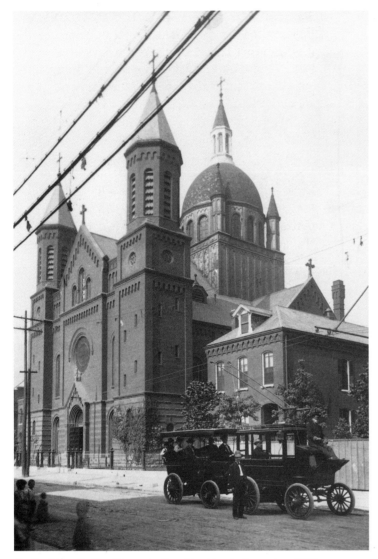

St. Stanislaus Kostka. Demonstration of trackless trolley system, 1903. Missouri Historical Society.

cultivated a strong ethnic identity while maintaining good relations with the Archdiocese. Construction of the new church began in 1891. The parish incorporated in the state of Missouri that same year, giving its Board of Directors – rather than the Archdiocese – control of the property, thus solving a problem that vexed Polish parishes in other American cities.

St. Stanislaus' design, described by contemporaries as "Byzantine-Polish Romanesque," clearly was intended to evoke Polish Old World heritage. The Byzantine effect once conveyed by a copper-sheathed exterior dome (removed in 1912) is still felt in three interior pendentive domes. A marble side altar with relief panels and a bejewelled icon, was brought to the church by Father Stanowski from a monastery in Cracow, Poland. After a fire in 1929, the congregation installed new windows (some of which portrayed Polish saints) by parishioner Michael Olszewski. They also commissioned an apse painting copied from "Golgotha," a 1904 World's Fair panorama by Polish artist Jan Styka.

The parish lost its nineteenth-century neighborhood context in the 1950s through clearance for the Pruitt-Igoe housing project. After demolition of the housing complex in the 1970s, the parish became virtually isolated. In the face of these

31. St. Stanislaus Kostka Roman Catholic Church NR, CL

1415 N. Twentieth Street (at Cass Avenue)
1891: Wessbecher & Hummel, St. Louis

The first Polish parish in St. Louis, St. Stanislaus constructed a substantial brick church-school within two years after the parish's inception in 1880. This two-story building still stands along with an 1890s rectory immediately north of the twin-towered red brick church. Under the innovative and forceful leadership of Polish-born Father Urban Stanowski, a Franciscan of aristocratic origins who came to the parish in 1885, the parish

St. Stanislaus Kostka. Choir, c. 1900. Landmarks collection.

staggering challenges, the congregation began a successful fund drive resulting in a new roof and the renovation of the interior. Supported by Polish-Americans from all over the metropolitan area, St. Stanislaus celebrates its Polish heritage with polka masses and festivals and stands today as a living symbol of Polish immigration and achievement in America.

completed the two-story (north) unit of the present building, where the parish began worshipping in a second-story chapel finished with a handsome open-timbered ceiling. Built of St. Louis limestone, some of which was salvaged from the 1873 Gothic church by John Beattie on Beaumont Street, the chapel unit originally was intended to be the first component of a much more ambitious church.

St. Stanislaus Kostka, c. 1892. Photo: E. Boehl. St. Louis Public Library.

32. St. Stephen's Lutheran Church
St. George's Episcopal Church
515 Pendleton Avenue (at Olive Street)
1891: Tully & Clark, St. Louis

St. George's, the phoenix church of St. Louis, rose from the ashes to build this English Gothic church after fire destroyed the congregation's church at Chestnut and Beaumont in 1891. Plans to relocate to a newer West End neighborhood were already under discussion before fire settled the question. Within a year, St. George's

Published in 1891, this design by Tully & Clark consisted of "four distinct buildings clustering around the massive square tower, 150 feet in height." The financial Panic of 1893 interrupted progress on that plan so that only the present modest-sized nave enlarged the chapel unit. The scale and the low horizontal lines of both designs follow an English parish church model rather than the cathedral type of the earlier Gothic Revival period. Inside, a low-sprung hammerbeam ceiling dominates the nave. Other examples of fine wood craftsmanship – oak pews, pulpit, communion rail, and altarpiece – enrich the sanctuary. Chancel fittings, including an elaborate carved wood reredos, date to the 1930s.

Organized in 1845 as a low church movement from Christ Church (#6), St. George built its first church in 1847 on Locust near Seventh Street. The building was a Neo-classical design by George I. Barnett. By the 1920s, financial problems caused the parish to consider a merger; in 1928, St. George turned over its property and merged with St. Michael and All Angels Church in St. Louis county (now St. Michael

St. Stephen's Lutheran, 1987. Photo: Landmarks Association, Cynthia Hill Longwisch.

Drawing: St. George's Episcopal, <u>American Architect and Building News</u>, Dec. 12, 1891. St. Louis Public Library.

and St. George). Many parishioners already had transferred there. In 1930, the Pendleton and Olive Street church was sold to St. Stephen's Lutheran for $29,500. St. Stephen's was organized in January 1930 as the result of efforts by Dr. Walter A. Maier of Concordia Seminary and the Student Missionary Society from the seminary. Support for the congregation from the Lutheran Church Missouri Synod has continued over the course of the past sixty-five years. In the late 1980s, the Lutheran Charities Foundation helped finance a new roof for the historic structure. Although the congregation today numbers fewer than fifty members, St. Stephen's maintains a grade school that attracts over sixty children.

Architect Kivas Tully (1852-1915), an Episcopalian born and schooled in Toronto, Canada, trained in Chicago. In partnership (1886-1910) with Charles W. Clark, he designed St. Peter's Episcopal Church (once at Spring and Lindell) and, in 1910, the tower, reredos, altar, and bishop's chair for Christ Church Cathedral (#6).

Berea Presbyterian, 1990. Photo: Landmarks Association, Cynthia Hill Longwisch.

Episcopal Church of the Redeemer, c. 1894. Photo: E. Boehl. Missouri Historical Society.

33. Berea Presbyterian Church
Episcopal Church of the Redeemer
3010 Olive Street (at Cardinal Avenue)
1892: John G. Cairns, St. Louis

When an 1891 fire destroyed St. George's Episcopal Church at Chestnut and Beaumont (see #32), the part of the congregation that wished to remain in the neighborhood organized Church of the Redeemer. The new Redeemer parish deviated from a strong Gothic Revival tradition of St. Louis Episcopal

churches by constructing the denomination's only Romanesque Revival-style building and the only non-Gothic church built before the modern period. A sweeping half-circle arch defines the original entrance facing Pine Street. Renovations in 1962 reoriented the entrance, which is now located on Olive Street. The interior of the church features an open-trussed ceiling in a design similar to Architect Cairns' other churches of the period.

Within a decade of the cornerstone-laying in 1892, the Redeemer congregation sold the church to the First Spiritualist Association and moved to the Central West End. In 1910, it merged with St. James parish. St James' contributions to the merger included a stone church built in 1900 at the corner of Cote Brilliante and Goode. That structure was moved at the time of the merger to the corner of Washington and Euclid where it continues to house the united parishes, renamed Trinity Episcopal in 1935.

Berea Presbyterian Church, a black congregation previously named Leonard Avenue Presbyterian, bought the old Redeemer church on Olive Street in 1908. Berea was the only one of forty-three churches to survive the massive Mill Creek Valley demolitions for urban renewal in the early 1960s. The congregation wanted to move when clearance began, but the St. Louis Presbytery persuaded them to remain and gave them money to remodel and enlarge the building. The Presbytery also recruited white families from other Presbyterian churches. These families became loan members of Berea and worked with the congregation during the difficult Mill Creek transition period. When LaClede Town (village-scale replacement housing) opened later that decade, Berea's congregation experienced additional integration in reverse. A 1995 feature story in the *Post-Dispatch*, "Farewell to Utopia," recounted meetings at the church leading to the formation of the New Democratic Coalition – a local "New Left" reform. Today, Berea once again faces the prospect of isolation as most of LaClede Town is scheduled for demolition.

34. The Church of St. Louis
Compton Hill Congregational Church
1640 S. Compton Avenue (at Lafayette Avenue)
1893: Warren H. Hayes, Minneapolis

Soon after its organization in 1881 as the Fifth Congregational Church, the members of this congregation began to seek for their church a more residential location than Clark and Twenty-third Streets. They selected a site at Compton and Lafayette in an emerging neighborhood close to exclusive Compton Heights (laid out 1888-90), where they took the name Compton Hill Congregational Church. A brick chapel was completed at the new site in 1888.

A drawing by local architect Theodore C. Link for a Compton Hill Congregational

The Church of St. Louis, 1995. Photo: Landmarks Association, Cynthia Hill Longwisch.

Drawing: Compton Hill Congregational, 1891. St. Louis Public Library.

Church was published in *American Architect* in early 1891. This was possibly a church for another city. In any case, the plan was not realized. The congregation turned to out-of-town talent for an 1893 design. Constructed of rock-faced limestone trimmed with wide bands of smooth stone, the Romanesque Revival church is typical of architect Warren H. Hayes' published designs for many Midwest and East Coast churches. The highly functional octagonal auditorium plan emphasizes good acoustics, sight lines, and expandable space. Curved pews in a fan-shaped arrangement on a sloping floor are directed to a tiered chancel with an elevated pulpit and choir stalls. Originally, a partition wall of movable doors (now covered) opened the auditorium to the adjoining chapel to accommodate overflow crowds. None of the original stained glass remains; replacement glass by Emil Frei (St. Louis) dates to the 1950s.

In 1955, Compton Hill Congregational Church merged with Mount Hope Evangelical and moved to the latter's church building at 3661 DeTonty Street. The building was purchased by the Christian Fundamental Church, organized by Joseph L. Autenrieth in the 1940s. The congregation later adopted its current name, the Church of St. Louis. In recent years, a small group of dedicated members has taken on the challenge of restoring the church to its original design.

Hayes began his practice in Elmira, New York, after graduating from Cornell University in 1871. His office was in Minneapolis from 1881 until his death in 1899. Hayes' other St. Louis project was the former Hyde Park Congregational Church (1894) at Bremen and Blair Streets in the Hyde Park neighborhood.

35. Cote Brilliante Presbyterian Church
4687 Labadie Avenue (at Marcus Avenue)
1894: Weber & Groves, St. Louis

This congregation began as an interdenominational chapel and Sunday school. By 1875, it occupied a board-and-batten Gothic edifice on the present site. Designed by Charles B. Clarke, the building featured classrooms in the arm of the cruciform plan. Methodist philanthropist

Union Chapel, c. 1890. Mercantile Library.

Samuel Cupples donated the land and served as school superintendent.

The building was called Union Chapel. By 1879, the name changed to Cote Brilliante Church. After a congregational vote to become Presbyterian, the St. Louis Presbytery organized a denominational church in 1885 and wisely appointed Cupples a Trustee.

Ground was broken in 1894 for a new $30,000 church of buff brick with terra cotta trim. The interior was not finished until the 1904 dedication. The plan followed an Akron-auditorium type: Sunday school rooms opened through sliding doors to the main auditorium which was articulated with an open-timbered ceiling. A massive 22-foot tower with heavily buttressed corners provided an entry vestibule. A photograph of this English Gothic church was published in the *Inland Architect* in 1900.

Substantial black in-migration and white flight during the World War II era dramatically changed many St. Louis neighborhoods. In an effort to stay the trend, the Cote Brilliante

Church Session, together with the Marcus Avenue Improvement Association, unsuccessfully petitioned the St. Louis Board of Education to prevent the Cote Brilliante public school from being assigned to blacks. Meanwhile, down the street at 4600 Labadie, the J. D. Shelley house, which had been purchased by a

Cote Brilliante Presbyterian, 1990. Photo: Landmarks Association, Cynthia Hill Longwisch.

black family in 1939, was a key element in the 1948 U.S. Supreme Court decision ending restrictive real estate covenants based on race (Shelley v. Kramer).

A dwindling white congregation at Cote Brilliante resisted relocation and, as did many congregations in other denominations, refused to integrate. In 1956, the St. Louis Presbytery assumed jurisdiction over the church and the all-white congregation dispersed. The church reopened a few months later under the same name with a policy of neighborhood outreach and service, especially to youth.

36. Zion Lutheran Church NRD
Zion German Evangelical Lutheran Church
2500 N. Twenty-first Street (at Benton Street)
1895: Albert Knell, St. Louis

The growth in affluence among north St. Louis German Lutherans within a single generation can be measured by comparing Zion Lutheran's first church with its second. The first, a vernacular two-story brick church-school (#9), was built in 1860 for approximately $8,000. The second, an imposing Gothic stone building designed to seat 1,270, cost over $100,000. As was often the practice of St. Louis German churches, Zion entrusted the building of the church to an architect and a contractor of German heritage. Raised in Europe, architect Albert Knell trained in Zurich and Stuttgart; contractor J. H. Drees belonged to the German Lutheran church.

The church exterior is

Zion Lutheran, 1995. Photo: Landmarks Association, Cynthia Hill Longwisch.

embellished with carved stone fashioned into pinnacles, pierced parapets, and ogee arches typical of English Decorated Gothic. Inside, the auditorium ceiling follows the shape of the gabled roof; plaster ribs mark the division of window bays. A balcony is located above the main entrances. Original marble and onyx religious furnishings, executed by north side sculptors Schrader & Conradi, include an elaborate Gothic pinnacled altarpiece depicting "The Ascension," a pulpit with images of the Evangelists, a baptismal font, and a reading stand. A Gothic-detailed stone parsonage connected to the church on the Benton Street side was completed in 1895.

Zion's records of English-language Sunday services illustrate a typical process of Americanization in German churches. In 1888, English-language services were only offered once a month in the evening. By 1905, they were held every Sunday. Although one German service was offered for older members each Sunday until 1942, the congregation gradually lost German-American members to outlying districts. Those who replaced them were the new immigrants: first Italian and Polish, then African-Americans. As the area changed, Zion placed greater emphasis on outreach missions to a congested, transient neighborhood. The 1995 parish census encompassed 188 households; the school closed in the early 1990s.

37. Centennial Christian Church NRD
Aubert Place Congregational Church
4950 Fountain Avenue (at Aubert Street)
1895: Grable, Weber & Groves, St. Louis

Picturesquely situated on the curve of an elliptical park platted in 1857, the Aubert Place Congregational Church building is constructed of grey brick in a Lombard Romanesque Revival style and features a characteristic tall campanile. White terra cotta ornamentation of Byzantine inspiration is concentrated around the triple-arch entrance. Above, the unusual gable trim displays corbels of alternating female and amphibian heads. The pattern is

Centennial Christian. **Photo: Robert C. Pettus, 1995.** *Landmarks Association.*

repeated on the western and southern gables. The interior follows an Akron-auditorium plan with a large centralized auditorium opening through wooden, vertical sliding doors into rectangular meeting rooms. A dramatic tent-like effect is created by a hammerbeam ceiling which springs from the floor to a center king post. Four small stained glass windows surround the king post. The building's design is

Centennial Christian. **Photo: Robert C. Pettus, 1995.** *Landmarks Association.*

Curby Memorial Presbyterian Church, 1990. Photo: Landmarks Association, Cynthia Hill Longwisch.

closely related to that of an 1897 south side church, Curby Memorial Presbyterian at Utah Street and Texas Avenue. Both were designed by the same architectural firm.

Aubert Place Congregational Church was organized in 1890. When construction began on the present church in 1895, Aubert Place merged with Third Congregational Church and the united churches adopted a new name: Fountain Park Congregational Church. Later mergers (1918-19) brought United Congregational and Plymouth Congregational into the Fountain Park Church, which nonetheless closed its doors by 1936. Next, First Christian Church (the parent organization of the St. Louis denomination) occupied the building. Less than a decade later, in 1945, Centennial Christian

Church (a black congregation founded in 1904) purchased the church.

38. Grace Methodist Church CHD
Lindell Avenue Methodist Episcopal Church
340 N. Skinker Boulevard (at Waterman Boulevard)
1896: Theodore C. Link (Link, Rosenheim & Ittner), St. Louis
1913: Frederick C. Bonsack, St. Louis

One of two or three St. Louis churches reconstructed stone by stone on a new site, Lindell Avenue Methodist Church (1892 chapel and 1896 main body) originally stood on the southwest corner of Lindell and Newstead across from the New Cathedral (#56). Between 1913 and 1914, the old church was torn down (chapel first) and

Grace Methodist, 1942. Mercantile Library.

Grace Methodist, 1930. Mercantile Library.

reerected, "the top stones of the old church becoming the bottom stones of the new church," according to Frederick C. Bonsack, architect for the reconstruction. Rededication as Grace Methodist Episcopal Church took place on October 11, 1914.

The auditorium, rebuilt following the original design, is defined by four expansive, round arches springing from short clustered columns. Dramatic plaster fan vaulting articulates the ceiling. Hand-carved pews of black birch are arranged amphitheater-style. An unusual proscenium arch features a plaster bas-relief with life-size figures depicting "The Glorification of the Virgin," executed by sculptor Robert P. Bringhurst (St. Louis). Window tracery is of Bedford limestone. Memorial art glass windows include "He Ascended Into Heaven" by Tiffany (New York); "Angel of Annunication" by Jacoby Art Glass Co. (St. Louis); and "Virgin and Child" by Emil Frei Co. (St. Louis). A marble baptismal font carved in Rome employs a conceit using the names of Violet and Marguerite (daughters of donor John W. Kauffman) in intertwined marble flowers on its base.

39.   Most Holy Trinity Roman Catholic Church   CL, CHD
3519 N. Fourteenth Street (at Mallinckrodt Street)
1897: Joseph Conradi, St. Louis

Holy Trinity's founding and location are linked directly to subdivision development in what once comprised the small community of New Bremen north of the city limits. In 1850, owners of Farrar's Addition offered Archbishop Kenrick a large parcel of land at North Fourteenth and Mallinckrodt Streets in hope of promoting German settlement. The donation was made on the condition that Kenrick build a German Catholic church and school on the site within six months. Holy Trinity's first brick church and school were completed that year. In 1898, Most Holy Trinity, St. Louis' third German-language parish, looked to Strasbourg Cathedral for a "German design" that would overshadow the impressive churches already constructed by its four daughter parishes. The mother church, a large, north side German Catholic parish founded in 1848, was still conducting services at its original site but in a modest second building erected in 1856. According to parish records, the congregation agreed that any new building should be a "splendid edifice, one that even after a century would still be proof of the faith and sacrifice of

Most Holy Trinity, 1979. Photo: Landmarks Association, Jill R. Johnson.

Most Holy Trinity, 1979. Photo: Landmarks Association, Jill R. Johnson.

Most Holy Trinity, c. 1900. Landmarks collection.

Christ. One is located above the central doorway; the other is inside above the north transept. Anthony Wallis Ornamental Stained Glass (St. Louis) executed the stained glass. George Pickel & Sons provided stone sculpture. Other finishes were supplied by St. Louis German firms, including some parishioners.

Parish descriptions of the completed church proudly noted the high quality of materials and methods of construction which, they boasted, made Holy Trinity "one of the strongest structures of modern architecture." Walls of Bedford limestone were combined with a heavy steel-frame floor and reinforced concrete slabs in the auditorium. Iron pillars strengthened 215-foot twin towers. After the 1927 tornado, most apse walls required reconstruction. A new marble high altar (modeled after the New Cathedral's), new confessionals, and a marble communion rail replaced tornado-damaged furnishings.

Plans for Holy Trinity were drawn by Joseph Conradi (1867-1936), an architect-sculptor who was born in Berne, Switzerland. Conradi studied art in Florence and Rome before coming to the United States in the late 1880s. After teaching at The Cooper Union in New York City, he moved to St. Louis where he formed a partnership with marble cutter Theodore Schrader. The firm, specialists in church altars and sculpture, received numerous commissions from Irish and German parishes. During the 1890s, Conradi turned to church architecture, working first in St. Louis, and then in St. Joseph, Missouri, and in the states of Louisiana, Idaho, Washington, and Utah. Conradi moved to the West Coast around 1916. Prominent examples of his sculpture may be found in many western cities, including all the sculpture in the Doheny Memorial Library at the University of Southern California in Los Angeles.

the people of Holy Trinity Parish." Members committed $100,000 to the construction of the new church. They also arranged that the west end be erected first so they could worship in its completed basement while work progressed on the eastern section.

Strasbourg Cathedral provided precedent for the use of a "mixed style": The lower church was designed in a "strictly Romanesque" style, while the upper church reflected an "early Gothic" one. Before a 1927 tornado, Holy Trinity also boasted a prominent octagonal crossing tower recalling Strasbourg's tower. The interior of Holy Trinity departs from the hall-plan of its four branch churches by the introduction of triforium and clerestory levels as in the Strasbourg model. Two notable statue groups depict a type of Pieta or *Not Gottes* in which God holds the limp body of

St. John Nepomuk, 1978. Landmarks collection.

40. St. John Nepomuk Roman Catholic Church NRD, CL

1631 S. Eleventh Street (at Lafayette Avenue)
1897: Architect unknown

With its founding in 1854, this parish became the first national church of Bohemian Catholics in the United States and reportedly the first to be built outside the mother country (now the Czech Republic). The parish grew into a center of Czech culture and a model for parishes around the country under the charismatic leadership of Father Joseph Hessoun. Born in Bohemia in 1830, Father Hessoun served at St. John's from 1865 until his death in 1906.

The cornerstone of the present Gothic Revival, red brick, hall-plan church was laid March 21, 1897, almost ten months after a tornado destroyed the previous 1870 building designed by Adolphus Druiding. The current building closely follows the original design (even reusing some of the original materials), but extends some 38 feet longer and employs new buff brick trim on the facade. The interior is richly furnished with wood statues, some from Bohemia, salvaged after the tornado. Columns of the nave arcade carry statues on pedestals. Other religious art dates from a later period: windows from Emil Frei's Munich studio (1929), stations of the cross from Bohemia (ca. 1930), and marble statues of SS. Wenceslaus and John Nepomuk (installed in 1938). An assemblage of other parish buildings remaining near the church testifies to the growth of the Bohemian Catholic community: an 1869 west school, an 1878 rectory, an 1884 east school, an 1887 convent, and an 1892 parish hall on the corner of Twelfth Street.

Before they established their own independent parishes, St. John Nepomuk ministered to several other ethnic groups in south St. Louis including Poles, Slovaks, Croatians, Slovenes, Lithuanians, and Hungarians. In spite of the

St. John Nepomuk, c. 1900. Photo: E. Boehl.
Missouri Historical Society.

population decline that began in the 1920s and the clearance of much of what was "Bohemian Hill" for public housing projects, St. John Nepomuk survived. It is still open today. Many worshippers come from outlying neighborhoods for homecoming and ethnic events. Midnight Mass on Christmas Eve was still in Czech as late as the mid-1970s. In 1988, the newer of the school buildings was recycled as condominiums.

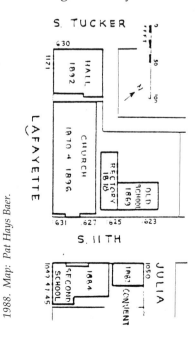

41. Trinity Lutheran Church NRD, CHD
Trinity German Evangelical Lutheran Church
1805 S. Eighth Street (at Soulard Street)
1896: Architect unknown

A tornado swept through the Soulard neighborhood on May 27, 1896, destroying Trinity's Gothic Revival brick church built in 1865. Reconstruction began the same year. The congregation was able to salvage a pulpit and a baptismal font from the 1865 sanctuary. Although the new church generally followed the first building's cruciform design with a tower centered in

Trinity Lutheran. **Photo: Robert C. Pettus, 1973.**
Landmarks Association.

the brick corbel-trimmed gable, the replacement church was smaller and the new spire was about 25 feet shorter than the original. The present rectory fills space occupied by old Trinity's long nave. An open auditorium plan without columns was substituted for the original Gothic nave arcade. A two-story brick school south of the church was also under construction in 1896 from plans by Charles F. May, who most likely served as architect for the church reconstruction. The school was enlarged in 1926.

Founded in 1839, Trinity is the mother church of all St. Louis Missouri Synod Lutheran churches. Trinity's first pastor, Otto Herman

Trinity German Evangelical Lutheran, c. 1865. St. Louis Public Library.

Walther's death in 1887 and the dissolution of the *General-gemeinde*, Trinity, Immanuel (#65), Holy Cross (#14), and Zion (#9 and 36) became independent congregations.

Today's congregation numbers almost 400 adults, some of whom continue to send their children to Trinity's elementary school which originated on the Saxon emigrant ship.

42. St. Teresa of Avila Roman Catholic Church

2413 N. Grand Avenue (at N. Market Street)
1899: Architect unknown

With its austere stone exterior and generous front lawn distancing the church from busy North Grand Avenue, St. Teresa of Avila today conveys the same contrast between the sacred and the secular world that was noted earlier by a turn-of-the-century journalist. The Catholic *Western Watchman* found the church's "Romanesque style a relief from the monotony of Gothic." Others described it as modified Romanesque with small domes typical of Roman basilicas. Indeed, the actual design drew on both Romanesque Revival and Italian Renaissance sources. According to the *Western Watchman*, parishioner Patrick Mulcahy, superintendent of construction, personally selected limestone "as will not readily absorb dampness and dust," explaining that "by this precaution the church will retain whiteness for a longer period than the average limestone building." Four decades and much urban grime later, sandblasting restored its "snowy whiteness."

Walther, came to Missouri with a group of Saxon Germans who immigrated in 1838-39. A majority of them settled in Perry County. Those who remained in St. Louis organized Trinity. Carl Ferdinand Wilhelm Walther succeeded his older brother as Trinity's pastor in 1842 and became a leading figure in the German-American Lutheran church. He devised a system of local church governance (*Generalgemeinde*) wherein satellite District Churches remained under his administration and supervision. Following the younger

St. Teresa of Avila, c. 1890. Photo: E. Boehl. Archdiocesan Archives.

Glass. In the organ loft, a "policemen's window," donated by parish members of the police force, once portrayed a "mailed and booted warrior" (St. Louis, King of France). The window is now gone.

Founded in 1865, the parish quickly erected its first church in "Byzantine style" on the present corner parcel. The names of early priests and parishioners indicate it was an Irish parish. At the laying of the cornerstone for the new church on June 3, 1900, the *Missouri Republican* reported that 2,400 people took part in a parade and 25,000 people attended the ceremony. The crowd might have been even greater, had a streetcar strike not stranded many Catholics living in remote parishes. Church cornerstone and dedication ceremonies commonly drew community-wide participation in the nineteenth and early twentieth centuries. These expressions of ecumenical spirit and pride were also occasions for elaborate, sometimes day-long, celebrations. Newspapers devoted lengthy columns to reporting on festivities, detailing sermons, music, people, and activities. Often, scant attention was given to the building itself.

Inside, an imposing nave with colonnade creates a monumental space heightened by elaborate ceiling paintings done on canvas. The paintings, apparently installed over a period of years, incorporate both Old and New Testament iconography. Matching classically detailed marble side altars flank a circa 1920 high altar where a rich display of mosaic work shows the influence of the New Cathedral's (#56) extensive mosaic decoration. St. Teresa's canopied altar features a mosaic figural group depicting Christ with symbols of the Eucharist. Parish pride claimed that all parts of the building had been "made in St. Louis." However, reports varied as to the local manufacturer of its "Munich style" stained glass windows: the recently established Emil Frei Co. or E. F. Kerwin Ornamental

St. Teresa of Avila, c. 1907. Photo: E. Boehl. Missouri Historical Society.

St. Teresa of Avila, 1990. Photo: Landmarks Association, Cynthia Hill Longwisch.

manesque Revival style. His successor firm – Shepley, Rutan & Coolidge – designed the 1896 chapel which displays typical Richardsonian round-arch motifs. Architectural quotations from Richardson's famous Trinity Church in Boston can be found in Second Presbyterian's prominent octagonal crossing tower and in its barrel-vaulted interior design. Bands of fine rusticated stonework recall architect Theodore Link's 1894 Union Station downtown.

The church boasts a noteworthy collection of stained glass by Tiffany Studios (New York). The company supplied a total of eleven windows. Six were installed by 1900; the remainder in the teens and early 1920s. The early windows earned praise in 1903 when the *St. Louis Republican* described them as "in keeping with the sumptuousness of

In the mid-1960s, St. Teresa's was placed under the pastoral care of the Montfort Fathers, a New York-based order dedicated to urban missionary work. When they arrived, the Fathers found St. Teresa's among the poorest parishes in the city. Additional aid came in the late 1970s when Mother Teresa of Calcutta established a small community of sisters near the church to work among the needy. On one of her visits to St. Louis, the Nobel Peace Prize laureate addressed a crowd of 900 assembled in the church, urging them to help the poor of the city. Today, the predominantly black parish boasts an attendance of 200 to 300 each Sunday, with many worshippers coming from outlying suburbs.

43. Second Presbyterian Church NR, CL, CHD

4501 Westminster Place (at Taylor Avenue)
1896: Shepley, Rutan & Coolidge, Boston
1899: Theodore C. Link, St. Louis

Second Presbyterian's chapel and church show the strong influence of Boston architect H. H. Richardson's interpretation of the Ro-

Tiffany window, installed 1922. Second Presbyterian Church Archives.

Second Presbyterian. **Photo: Robert C. Pettus, 1975.** *Landmarks Association.*

population trend, the Presbyterians selected a new location at Taylor and Westminster in the developing Central West End. They first worshipped in the stone Romanesque Revival chapel now attached to the west end of the main church. It was designed by Shepley, Rutan & Coolidge. An education building by LaBeaume & Klein (St. Louis) enlarged the church facilities in 1930. Electing not to move further west in the 1960s, the congregation has remained active in neighborhood preservation and social services. A million-dollar endowment fund helps maintain these programs and the immense physical plant.

this home of one of the most fashionable congregations of St. Louis. The cost was from $3,500 down to $1,300 a window." These fees were well above the average $300 per window for turn-of-the-century churches.

The congregation, an 1838 colony from First Presbyterian Church, built its first church at Broadway (then Fifth) and Walnut Street in 1840. The brick Greek Revival church was designed by Lucas Bradley (St. Louis). A move to Sixteenth and Walnut, planned for 1864, never took place because of the withdrawal of a large conservative faction of the congregation. Instead, this group moved into the new building and became the Sixteenth Street Presbyterian Church (see #19 and #62). Three years later, Second Church purchased a better lot at Seventeenth and Locust Streets. Their new Gothic Revival church at this location was designed by Randolph Brothers and featured a celebrated all-stone spire. The building joined the company of other prominent Lucas Place institutions and fine residences. The sole survivor of this once-fashionable district is the Campbell House Museum, the former home of Second Presbyterian members Robert G. Campbell and family.

In 1896, following the familiar westward

44. Lafayette Park United Methodist Church NRD, CHD
Lafayette Park Methodist Episcopal, South
2300 Lafayette Avenue (at Missouri Avenue)
1887; 1900: William A. Cann, St. Louis

The lineage of this congregation reaches back to 1840 and a south St. Louis mission that grew first into Wesley Chapel (1843-48), then Chouteau Avenue Methodist Church (1850-87). By the 1880s, Chouteau Methodist's once prestigious location at Eighth and Chouteau had passed its prime, and the congregation began a search for a better address. They selected stylish Lafayette Park, one of the city's finest districts, which already claimed congregations of Baptists, Unitarians, Episcopalians, and Presbyterians.

An 1884 Sunday School near the present church site sowed the seed for the Methodist congregation. Financed by members of several other Methodist churches, a limestone chapel facing Missouri Avenue was under way in

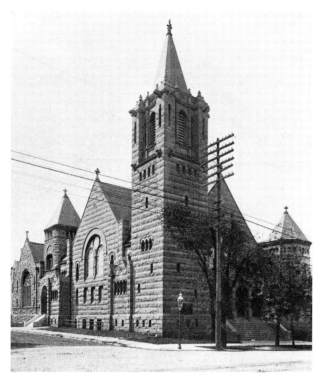

Lafayette Park United Methodist, 1901. Missouri Historical Society.

seven churches for Methodist and Presbyterian congregations here. He was a member of two of the Methodist churches that he designed: Lafayette Park and, later, Fry Memorial Methodist (1905) in Clifton Heights. At his death in 1912 at age 49, he was credited with more than 600 church designs across the country.

HOLY CORNERS

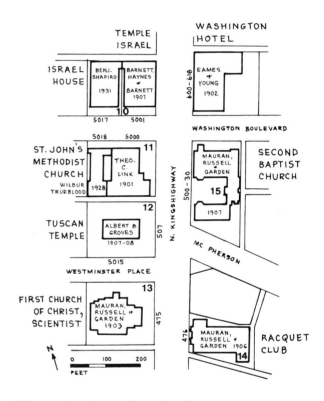

1988. Map: Pat Hays Baer for Landmarks Association.

1887. All four churches in the Lafayette Park neighborhood were unroofed by the 1896 tornado. Repairs were complete by the time the Methodists laid the cornerstone for their main building in September 1900.

The complex is distinguished by fine Richardsonian Romanesque stonework in alternating courses of rock- and smooth-faced limestone. Carved stone foliated capitals, some with cherub heads, enrich short clustered columns on the Lafayette Avenue entrance arcade; gargoyles and beasts accent the tower. Inside, an octagonal auditorium follows a popular Protestant plan type modeled after theater designs to improve acoustics and sight lines. Pews are arranged in a fan shape on an inclined floor; a projecting "performance" stage is created by a tiered chancel that elevates the pulpit and choir stalls. The top tier of this chancel displays elaborately stenciled organ pipes. Also recalling theater design are four small balconies that overlook the sanctuary and offer additional seating.

Born in Kentucky, architect William Cann moved to St. Louis with partner J. A. Lynch in 1894. Between 1900 and 1913, Cann designed

The tendency of prominent congregations to cluster in the central corridor during their 100-year march westward is illustrated by four turn-of-the-century churches that comprise the Holy Corners group in the Central West End. In the nineteenth century, these congregations occupied substantial buildings designed by leading architects located within a few blocks of one another on "Piety Hill." They drew together in even closer proximity when, one by one, within about five years, they moved to North Kingshighway in the heart of the city's exclusive private place residential area.

Stylistically, the group is notable for the absence of the ubiquitous Gothic Revival style that remained the mainstay of most St. Louis church-building well into the twentieth century. The strong presence of Classical forms in Holy Corners derives in part from the popularity of an architectural image established by the buildings of two World's Fairs: Chicago in 1893 and St. Louis in 1904. Religious houses on the west side of Kingshighway display an impressive progression of Classical orders beginning with the Doric (Christian Science), then Ionic (St. John's), and ending with Corinthian (Temple Israel).

All four groups fostered sound interfaith relationships in the nineteenth century while located on "Piety Hill." They continued to cultivate an ecumenical spirit in the twentieth century. St. John's Methodist and First Christ, Scientist, have elected to stay in Holy Corners; the other two congregations remained there into the 1950s and 1960s.

45. St. John's Methodist Church NR, CL
St. John's Methodist Episcopal Church
5000 Washington Avenue (at N. Kingshighway Boulevard)
1901: Theodore C. Link, St. Louis

St. John's pioneered the way to Kingshighway, breaking ground there in 1901. The congrega-

St. John's Methodist. **Photo: Robert C. Pettus, 1974.** *Landmarks Association.*

tion moved from an 1867 brick Gothic church (#12) at Locust and Ewing to a Classical Revival limestone church at the new site. It was dedicated on May 10, 1903. The building is articulated with fluted Ionic temple-fronts on two facades; an asymmetrically-placed campanile provides a distinctive vertical accent. St. John's centralized auditorium plan is arranged with fan-shaped seating below a fine coffered barrel vault ceiling. Full-figure portrait windows of John and Charles Wesley (the English founders of Methodism) are by Emil Frei (St. Louis). In 1945, plans drawn up by Study, Farrar & Majers (St. Louis) revamped the chancel with a coffered arch; Alfred Gass (St. Louis) carved a new altar, pulpit, choir stalls, and reredos; Siegfried Reinhardt (St. Louis) designed an altar window, "St. John of Patmos." Later, Rodney Winfield (St. Louis) created

St. John's Methodist. **Photo: Robert C. Pettus, 1974.** *Landmarks Association.*

St. John's Methodist. **Photo: Robert C. Pettus, 1974.**
Landmarks Association.

46. First Church of Christ, Scientist
NR, CL

477 N. Kingshighway Boulevard (at Westminster Place)
1903: Mauran, Russell & Garden, St. Louis

Founded in 1894 as one of the first five Christian Science churches in the world, this congregation became the first of eight organized by 1926 within the city of St. Louis. The first St. Louis church was built in 1895 on Pine near Leffingwell. Its modified Tudor Gothic design by Link, Rosenheim & Ittner (St. Louis) did not yet reflect the denomination's hallmark Classicism, a style that became the standard nationwide. Original plans of the Kingshighway building called for a $300,000 domed temple-front church, probably of stone. Revised to meet a budget of $100,000, the tan brick church reflected an Arts & Crafts interest in masonry and a relaxation of traditional Classical ornamentation. Ground breaking took place in September 1903; by the next summer, guests from the 1904 World's Fair were able to view the completed auditorium.

Several features introduced in the design of First Church were later adopted in other St. Louis Christian Science buildings: a central-plan auditorium located on an upper level, bowl-shaped seating on an inclined floor, restrained Classical interior decoration with a prominent center ceiling feature, large windows glazed with non-figural art glass in pale colors of delicate design, and flat or low-vaulted ceilings. Many of these features were intended to create optimum hearing and visibility of the reader's platform.

St. John's Methodist. **Photo: Robert C. Pettus, 1974.** *Landmarks Association.*

monochromatic windows executed by Emil Frei Associates. William Trueblood (St. Louis) designed the Education Building to the west in 1927.

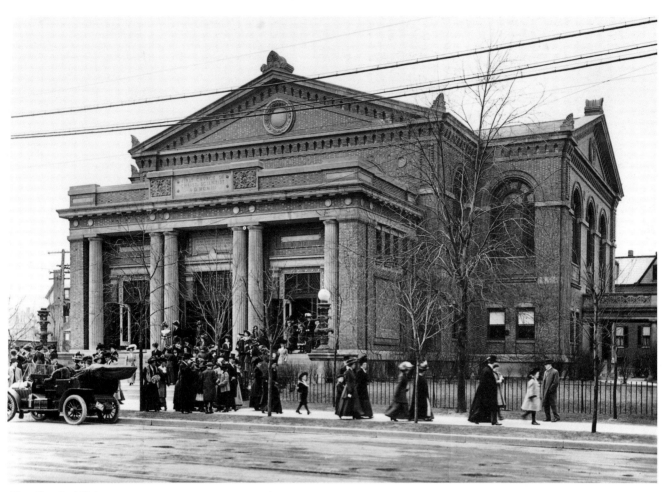

First Church of Christ,
Scientist, c. 1905.
Missouri Historical
Society.

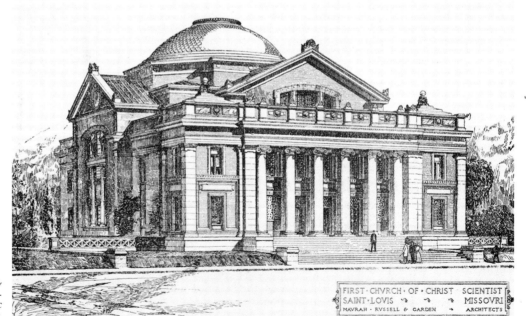

First Church of Christ,
Scientist, 1901.
St. Louis Public
Library.

Baptist Church of the Good Shepherd. **Photo: Robert C. Pettus, 1974.** *Landmarks Association.*

47. Baptist Church of the Good Shepherd NR, CL
Second Baptist Church
500 N. Kingshighway Boulevard (at Washington Boulevard)
1907: Mauran, Russell & Garden, St. Louis

In 1902, this congregation purchased land for what would become a *tour de force* of brick-work. Ground breaking took place in 1906. The complex embraces two gable-front units: a south education building marked by a large pointed-arch window and a north auditorium displaying an elaborate rose window. Front and rear loggias surrounding a garden area connect the units. Executed in the Medieval/ Renaissance brick design tradition of Lombardy in Northern Italy, the buildings exhibit an unusually artful use of materials in which color controls design. Resting on a foundation of dark red Missouri granite, brick walls rise in graduated hues ranging from purplish brown at the base to pale buff at the top. Mortar is uncolored Portland cement. Hand-ground bricks form major arches and provide ornamental accents; all the terra cotta trim is of custom design. Door jambs, sills, and columns employ Minnesota yellow sandstone; roofs are red tile. The interior of the north auditorium features a pointed-arch nave arcade of composition stone columns and an open truss ceiling.

An affluent congregation highly conscious of style, the members of Second Baptist chose among East Coast church designs for their 1873 building on "Piety Hill" (designed by New York architect C. L. Nichols). High style, however, presented a problem to some Baptists who renounced Second Baptist's formal services and Sunday dress code of morning coats and striped trousers for minister, choir, and male congregation members. Preferring a simpler mode, members of Beaumont Baptist vetoed a possible merger with Second Baptist, and formed Garrison Avenue Church (#21) instead. When Second Baptist moved to the Holy Corners site, it once again spared no expense. Its new church cost over $300,000. The 216-foot campanile (a gift of Francis H. Ludington) added $80,000 to the total cost. The tower lost its upper 60 feet in 1951 when declining church finances and membership could not support its maintenance. In 1954, the congregation sold the building and moved far west in St. Louis County.

Temple Israel, 1936. Mercantile Library.

48. Angelic Temple of Deliverance
NR, CL

Temple Israel
5001 Washington Boulevard (at N. Kingshighway Boulevard)
1907: Barnett, Haynes & Barnett, St. Louis

Temple Israel was organized in 1886 by prominent German Jews as a liberal offshoot of Shaare Emeth, St. Louis' first Reformed Jewish congregation. The group quickly built its first synagogue. Their 1887 building (since razed) by Grable & Weber (St. Louis) at Leffingwell and Pine Streets was one of the city's earliest examples of the Richardsonian Romanesque style – a mainstream Christian style. This set the synagogue apart from the nineteenth-century temple designs that evoked the exotic eastern origins of Judaism.

The congregation's later temple in Holy Corners, an impressive Corinthian-columned building of Caen stone, was based on a design reportedly derived from the Roman Temple of Vespasian. Remarks offered by congregation president Moses Fraley at the 1907 dedication expressed the proud place Temple Israel held on fashionable Kingshighway: "No longer as in dark European lands need we hide our sanctuaries in obscure alleys, or skulk timidly in ghettos."

In 1908, Temple Israel's address represented the most western of all St. Louis Jewish houses of worship; by 1950, it had become the most eastern of all Reform temples and of most Conservative and Orthodox congregations. A majority of members lived in or were en route to St. Louis county. Deciding to move to the county in 1953, this congregation purchased land in Ladue. In 1954, however, the Ladue Council denied the Temple's application to build, basing its decision on allegations that overcrowding would result at the site. The congregation then purchased a site in the city of Creve Coeur the same year. Construction was delayed again, until a 1959 Missouri Supreme Court decision upheld the right of religious freedom and affirmed the congregation's right to build despite the objections of Creve Coeur. Finally, in 1962, Temple Israel left Kingshighway for a new building at Ladue and Spoede Roads.

Temple Israel, 1936. Mercantile Library.

Temple Israel, 1936. Mercantile Library.

THE UNION BOULEVARD COLLECTION

During the years that the Kingshighway congregations moved west to form Holy Corners (#45-48), a similar migration was occurring along Union Boulevard a few blocks further west. Between 1904 and 1907 three congregations - Union Christian, Pilgrim Congregational, and Church of the Messiah Unitarian - erected corner churches in the 700-800 blocks of Union. In 1913, a fourth church, Westminster Presbyterian, joined the row, locating one block south at the corner of Delmar. Weber & Groves and Mauran, Russell & Garden, the two local firms responsible for the four Union Boulevard churches, had also drawn up plans for church and fraternal buildings in Holy Corners. Part of an impressive institutional lineup along Union, the churches neighbored (south to north) the Young Men's Hebrew Association (1927), the St. Louis Artists' Guild (1907), Soldan High School (1908), William Clark Elementary School (1906), and the Cabanne Branch of the St. Louis Public Library (1906).

The Church of the Messiah merged with another Unitarian congregation during the Depression and moved a few blocks away. Union Christian, Pilgrim Congregational, and Westminster Presbyterian maintained urban missions ministering to a changing neighborhood in the post-World War II era, successfully integrating in the 1950s and resisting flight to the suburbs.

49. Union Avenue Christian Church
CL, CHD

733 Union Boulevard
1904; 1907: Albert B. Groves (Weber & Groves), St. Louis

The first church to break ground on Union Boulevard (formerly Avenue), Union Christian erected a chapel on the present site in 1904. The main body of the 100 x 103-foot church was completed in 1908. Alternating bands of rough- and smooth-faced limestone enliven the walls; intricate Byzantine-style carved stone enriches the front arcade. Deep, round-arched corbel tables on the gables and a tall, slender campanile define the Northern Italian Romanesque style which architect Albert B. Groves had earlier introduced in two churches (see #37) in brick, a material more commonly employed with that style. The interior was

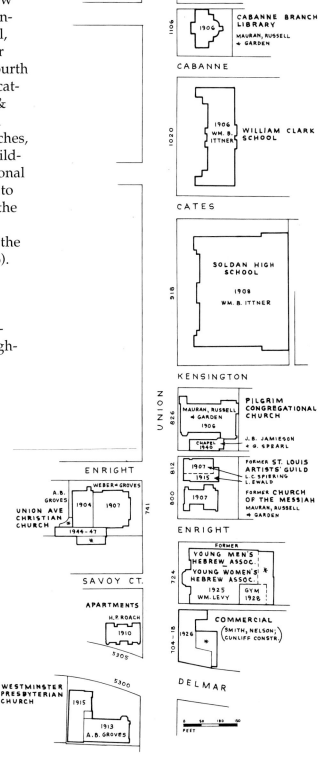

1995. Map: Pat Hays Baer.

remodeled in 1957 with new pews and a reconfigured chancel. Earlier changes added a woodcarving of "The Last Supper" by Anton Lang (1943), a member of the family famous for the Oberammergau Passion Play, and a new chapel (1947) with a modernistic stained-glass window by Emil Frei of St. Louis.

Union Christian traces its origin to 1871 when a group of First Christian Church members were dismissed after they insisted that organ music be added to the all-vocal worship services. The new congregation took the name Central Christian Church. In 1887, members erected a brick church at 3619 Finney near Grand, one of the two oldest church buildings of that denomination remaining in the city. In 1902, Central Christian merged with Mt. Cabanne Christian and moved into their building (since demolished) at Kingshighway and Enright. The congregation adopted the current name after relocating in the new chapel on Union.

Albert B. Groves (1868-1926), trained at Cornell University, designed (either alone or with partners Grable and Weber) twelve extant St. Louis churches. Six of these were Presbyterian.

Union Avenue Christian. Sanders & Melsheimer, engravers, c. 1908. Mercantile Library.

50 . Pilgrim Congregational United Church of Christ   CL, CHD
Pilgrim Congregational Church
826 Union Avenue
1906: Mauran, Russell & Garden, St. Louis

This church group was named for the Congregational English immigrants (separatists from the Church of England) who landed at Plymouth, Massachusetts, in December 1620. To commemorate this historic event, Congregationalists set aside December 22 as Forefathers Day. Pilgrim, following a typical founding pattern of St. Louis Protestant churches, began as a Sunday School in 1853. The school reorganized as a church in 1866 when construction of a stone chapel began on the corner of Ewing and Washington in "Piety Hill." Pilgrim chose

Pilgrim Congregational, c. 1910. Missouri Historical Society.

Forefathers Day for the dedication of that chapel as well as for the cornerstone-laying and dedication of an adjoining state-of-the-art Gothic church (1867) designed by Henry Isaacs (St. Louis). The church boasted a 230-foot steeple – 10 feet taller than that of First Presbyterian at Fourteenth and Lucas, making it the tallest in St. Louis (see page 10). It was greatly enhanced by

the gift of a set of chimes and a striking clock. These were later moved to the new church tower on Union Avenue.

The old bells, however, carried with them a legal proviso governing their use. In 1879, two "Piety Hill" residents found the bell-ringing "an intolerable nuisance" and filed suit. When the case came to trial, a host of church neighbors, including publisher Joseph Pulitzer, testified in defense of the chimes. In 1881, a compromise judgment restricted the clock's striking to daylight hours and permitted the carillon to play only "as a summons to religious worship."

Pilgrim's members, already gravitating westward at the turn of the century, deferred relocation of the church until after the St. Louis World's Fair. In 1904, they purchased the present site. The church proper, completed in 1907 of rock-faced pink granite trimmed with smooth white limestone introduced a Northern Italian Romanesque style which Union Christian (#49) echoed across the street. Pilgrim's handsome facade was further enriched with inlaid polychrome stone work. New doors installed in 1933 were designed by architect-designer Charles Eames, a member, who also drew up plans to rebuild the lightning-damaged tower in 1935. A Tudor Gothic chapel of matching pink granite designed in 1940 by Jamieson & Spearl (St. Louis) adjoins the south wall of the church.

Mauran, Russell & Garden designed six extant St. Louis churches including Pilgrim and the former Unitarian church one door south (#51). The architects' growing interest in the Arts & Crafts movement was visible in an expressive use of stone on the exterior and in a simple, straightforward handling of materials inside. The congregation acknowledged the contributions of craftsmen by including in the cornerstone box a photograph of masons and carpenters at work on the church.

Parrish Temple Christian Methodist Episcopal, 1991. Photo: Landmarks Association, Cynthia Hill Longwisch.

51. Parrish Temple Christian Methodist Episcopal Church CHD
Church of the Messiah Unitarian
800 Union Boulevard (at Enright Avenue)
1907: John L. Mauran (Mauran, Russell & Garden), St. Louis

This unassuming brick church received notice in an early twentieth-century publication promoting designs of small brick churches sponsored by the Hydraulic Brick Co. (St. Louis). Designed in Gothic Revival style, the church achieves much of its effect through artful use of building materials rather than elaborate ornament. Exterior walls display subtle brick masonry laid in English bond on the basement level; above that, brick is laid in Flemish bond with salt-glazed headers. A mottled green slate roof provides color contrast. Interior spaces also emphasize materials in exposed brick walls, natural wood floors, and a simple open-timbered ceiling.

A participant in the dedication service in 1907, Henry W. Eliot (father of T. S. Eliot and a founder of the Hydraulic Pressed Brick Co.) was a direct link to the congregation's origins and illustrious history. In 1834, his father, Reverend William Greenleaf Eliot (1811-87), organized the congregation (the first Unitarian church west of the Mississippi). Members became a prosperous, altruistic force in St. Louis, responsible for founding numerous cultural and educational institutions. Led by Eliot, all seventeen original incorporators of Washington University in 1853 held membership in the Church of the Messiah.

The congregation's earlier churches also represented distinguished designs. The second church at Ninth and Olive (1850, Gothic Revival) was reportedly the largest Protestant church in St. Louis at the time. The third church at Locust and Garrison on "Piety Hill" was a Peabody & Stearns (Boston) design which introduced the first important outside influence on St. Louis architecture. At the time of their move to Union Avenue, the congregation removed several windows from the Peabody & Stearns building and installed them in their fourth church.

A second Unitarian congregation, the Church of the Unity, built a modest stone church in 1870. Designed by local architect Frederick W. Raeder, that building still stands at a Park Avenue corner across from Lafayette Square. In 1917, Unity moved to a new church designed by William B. Ittner (St. Louis) at 5007 Waterman just south of Holy Corners (#45-48) on N. Kingshighway. Weakened by the Depression, Messiah and Unity voted to consolidate in 1938, adopted the name First Unitarian Church of St. Louis, and agreed to locate in the Waterman building.

In 1939, the Unitarians sold their Union Avenue church to Bible Presbyterian, a white congregation. When the latter group sold in 1953 to Parrish Chapel of the Colored Methodist Episcopal Church, racial tensions in the neighborhood ran high. Organized in 1920 by Reverend Thomas H. Parrish, Parrish Chapel (later Temple) began as a south St. Louis mission known as Crisk Chapel. The group moved in 1920 into a former Congregational church at 2407 Belle Glade Avenue where they worshipped until purchasing the present building. Today, Parrish is a welcome and active member of the Union Avenue Association of Churches, a group which sponsors ecumenical services and events.

Architect John Lawrence Mauran (1866 - 1933), was born in Providence, R.I., and graduated from M.I.T. in 1889. He joined the Boston office of Shepley, Rutan & Coolidge, who first sent him to Chicago to work on the Public Library and Art Institute there, and later (1893),

to St. Louis as the firm's representative. In 1900, he formed a partnership with Ernest J. Russell and Edward G. Garden, both of whom also worked for Shepley, Rutan & Coolidge. Mauran, a member of the congregation, served as President of the Board of Trustees of the Church of the Messiah when he designed the building. The pastor's words at its dedication expressed Mauran's special connection to the building: "We feel it is the work of our own hands and are correspondingly proud of it and attached to it." The Unitarians paid highest honor to Mauran in 1934 when they placed a bronze tablet in the church bearing the same epitaph as one over the tomb of architect Christopher Wren in St. Paul's Cathedral, London: "If you seek his monument, look around you."

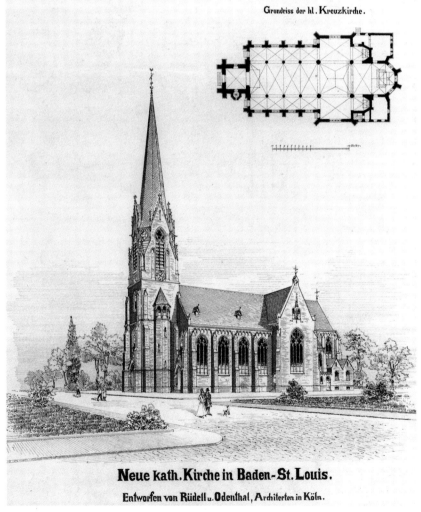

Holy Cross, c. 1903. Drawing: Landmarks collection.

Holy Cross, c. 1940. Missouri Historical Society.

52. Holy Cross Roman Catholic Church NR

8115 Church Road
1903: Rüdell & Odenthal, Cologne, Germany

German-American trust in Old World talent came to fruition in Holy Cross' red brick Gothic Revival hall-church with trilobal apse. Plans dated 1903-06 by Rüdell & Odenthal (Cologne) received close scrutiny and direction from Holy Cross rector Peter Wigger – the second in a Wigger dynasty of Westphalian priests whose 75-year tenure fostered parish solidarity. Considered the "great power" in the formative years, Father Wigger captured the parish spirit when he proclaimed: "Succeeding generations shall know who built this church. We did not solicit or beg from anyone outside our own parish. We are no beggars. We are Germans." (Schooled in the arts, Father Wigger entered a wood model of the new church in a 1904 World's Fair competition category for architectural engineering. He donated his $1,000 prize to the building fund.)

Carl Rüdell, architect and watercolorist, was born in Trier, Germany in 1855. A prominent designer of approximately eighty German churches, Rüdell has watercolor paintings in German museum collections. St. Louis sculptor-architect Joseph Conradi modified the original plans, supervised construction, and carved stone heads of angels and of Christ which embellish front entrances. Figural art glass is by the Emil Frei Studio, Munich. Reverend Wigger designed a white Italian marble altar executed by T. G. Schrader Sons (St. Louis). Gothic side altars with liturgical renewal iconography, planned in 1943 by Reverend Martin B. Hellriegel, incorporate lindenwood statues (1878) by Max Schneiderhahn (St. Louis); Gottfried Schiller (St. Louis) executed the altars.

Located in Baden, a north St. Louis district named for the birthplace of its early German settlers, the parish organized in 1864 as a mixed Irish-German congregation. After the Irish withdrew in 1872 to form Our Lady of Mt. Carmel a block away, Holy Cross became a

German national church. Monsignor Martin B. Hellriegel (1890 - 1981), the fourth in an uninterrupted line of German-born rectors, became pastor in 1940. Under his progressive leadership the parish gained international recognition as a pioneering center for liturgical reform well in advance of Vatican II. Holy Cross became a model of successful application of the liturgical apostolate at the parish level, attracting thousands of visitors, including many prominent figures in the movement from Europe and the United States. Holy Cross' working-class congregation today is a mosaic of ethnic origins including a few of the old German families.

Immaculate Conception, c. 1950. Archdiocesan Archives.

53. Immaculate Conception-St. Henry Roman Catholic Church
Immaculate Conception Roman Catholic Church
3120 Lafayette Avenue (at Longfellow Boulevard)
1904: Barnett, Haynes & Barnett, St. Louis

"Beautiful in its conception, beautiful in its execution, bearing in every line the beauty of Catholic architecture," pronounced Archbishop Glennon when he dedicated this church in 1908. Others lavished additional praise,

hailing it as "one of the finest Gothic structures in the West" and pointed to no less than three "magnificent rose windows" located in the facade and at both ends of the transept. The earliest of a group of five Catholic parish churches designed 1904-10 by Barnett, Haynes & Barnett, architects of the New Cathedral (#56), Immaculate Conception reveals a richly finished interior with ochre marble columns supporting a Gothic nave arcade with blind triforium and clerestory. "Alps green" marble wainscotting embellishes the walls.

Organized in 1876 under the name St. Kevin's in honor of Dublin's patron saint, the parish worshipped in two earlier churches (built 1876 and 1889) located a few blocks north of the present site. Changes in the neighborhood persuaded the Archdiocese that the new church should be built in a "more prominent location" adjoining the prestigious Compton Heights subdivision. The parish still bore St. Kevin's name when the cornerstone was laid in 1904. In addition to standard items (such as newspapers, coins, and parish archives), it also contained a timely memento: pictures of officers of the St. Louis World's Fair held that year.

At the dedication, Archbishop Glennon conferred a new title, Immaculate Conception, transferring the name of an early (1853) defunct parish originally located at Eighth and Chest-

Immaculate Conception, 1995. Photo: Landmarks Association, Cynthia Hill Longwisch.

nut. Glennon's decision to rename St. Kevin's was very likely formulated in 1904. The universal Catholic Church had just celebrated the 50th anniversary of Pope Pius IX's official proclamation of Immaculate Conception dogma. The archbishop's dedication sermon was captioned by the *St. Louis Republic*, "Home Depends on Women . . . Prelate Holds Up the Blessed Virgin as Exemplar of Perfect Home." Opening a new church honoring Mary's immaculate conception offered Glennon the occasion to express his conservative views on contemporary society: "There would be no skeletons in the closets of St. Louis homes if the purity and simplicity that formerly obtained were observed today." Glennon attributed the "decadence of [early twentieth-century] domestic standards to women's mad rush to satiate ambition and to indulge in vanities of the world."

Immaculate Conception merged with St. Henry (1230 California at Rutger) in 1977.

54. St. Augustine Roman Catholic Church

(St. Barbara's Roman Catholic Church)
5909 Minerva Avenue (at Hamilton Boulevard)
1905: Henry E. Peipers, St. Louis

In a sense, St. Barbara's was founded twice on the same site. It first appeared about 1878 in a small frame chapel staffed by Jesuits at Hamilton and Minerva. This mission church, subsequently named for St. Rose of Lima, served farmers and dairymen living in the undeveloped Rose Hill tract. In 1891, when planning a larger church, the parish decided to locate further east at Goodfellow and Etzel, where they constructed St. Rose's church (later replaced in 1909 by the building standing today). Meanwhile, German Catholics living in the same area had no church that offered services in their native tongue. To remedy this situation, the diocese

repurchased the original parcel in 1893 and organized St. Barbara's parish in the old frame chapel at Hamilton and Minerva.

The West End building boom generated by the 1904 World's Fair swelled the ranks of St. Barbara's. In a single year after the Fair, the rector reported that sixty new houses constructed near the church had pushed St. Barbara's past capacity. Continuing a nineteenth-century tradition of associating St. Louis German churches with medieval precedents in Germany, historian Rev. John Rothensteiner likened St. Barbara's new church to Frankfurt's Cathedral, in which the "coronations of the Roman Emperors of the German Nation were held." Characteristic of German congregations, the parish selected a German-born architect.

St. Barbara's, c. 1905. Photo: George Porrill. Private collection.

St. Barbara's, built for $40,000, did originally evoke the distinctive tower of the Cathedral of Frankfurt am Main; the St. Louis church no longer boasts its top stage. The hall-church interior displays an impressive Gothic nave arcade. With limited funds but an eye toward future growth, the parish completed the church without the large apse, later added (1927) from plans drawn up by Widmer Engineering Co. and architect Louis Preuss. In addition to the church, three other parish buildings appeared within a decade to accommodate the fast-growing congregation: a school (1908-12), a sisters' residence (1916), and hall (1917). The church updated the interior during the 1930s, trimming down altars and acquiring a new marble baptismal font, wrought iron gates, a new marble altar table, and new lighting fixtures.

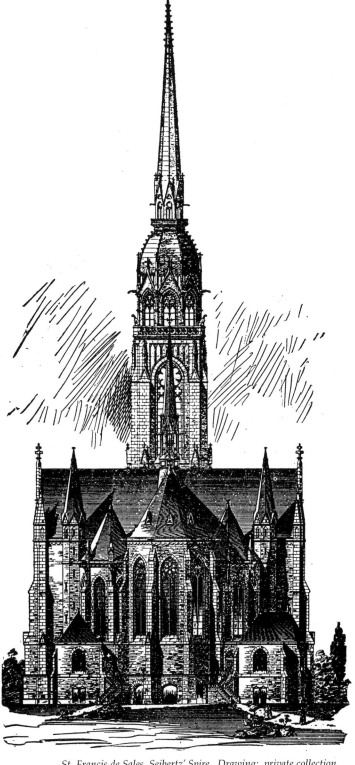

St. Francis de Sales, 1967. Photo: Al Guise. Landmarks Collection.

St. Francis de Sales, Seibertz' Spire. Drawing: private collection.

55. St. Francis de Sales Roman Catholic Church CL, NR

2653 Ohio Street (at Lynch Street)
1907: Victor Klutho (St. Louis) modified
1894 plans by Engelbert Seibertz (Berlin)

Strong cultural links of St. Louis Germans to the Fatherland played a prominent role in the building history of St. Francis de Sales, an ambitious daughter church of SS. Peter & Paul (#18). In 1894, according to parish records, de Sales rector John Peter Lotz, "determined to have the largest and finest church in the city," traveled to Berlin to consult with architect Seibertz. Two German churches reportedly inspired the plans Father Lotz brought back: St. Paul's Church and Dominican Cloister, an 1892 Gothic Revival design by Seibertz in Moabit (Berlin), and the Cathedral of Frankfurt am Main. The reports proved correct. St. Francis de Sales, as built, drew on St. Paul's plan, hall-church interior, and facade composition. Seibertz' unbuilt spire imitated that of the Frankfurt Cathedral.

Construction began in 1895. Financial difficulties interrupted work for more than a decade after an 1896 tornado ravaged parish homes and destroyed the 1867 brick church. The congregation roofed the completed basement of their new church and held services there for over ten years. Finally, building resumed in 1907,

and reached completion in 1908 under the direction of parishioner-architect Victor Klutho. Seibertz' design called for a stone church estimated at over $500,000. Klutho substituted less expensive grey mottled brick and terra cotta, but parish pride insisted that a 300-foot steel-frame spire be completed despite budget strains. Reward for their hopes of making a big statement came when flattering press declared the height of the church nave to be equal to seven stories of the new Frisco office building

St. Francis de Sales, c. 1960. Landmarks collection.

downtown, and its spire to be twice as tall as the same building. Church historian Reverend John Rothensteiner offered the highest accolade when he called St. Francis the "crown of the later Gothic churches, vying with St. Alphonsus, SS. Peter & Paul, St. Francis Xavier and Holy Trinity for the palm of glorious Christian architecture."

Wegener Bros., a south side firm, executed the brickwork; Winkle Terra Cotta Co. (St. Louis) manufactured window tracery and other ornament. Emil Frei, Sr. crafted the art glass images of saints. Wood dominates the interior furnishings. E. Hackner of La Crosse, Wisconsin provided the reredos and communion rail; Lausberg & Macke of Louisville executed four smaller altars, confessionals, and pews. Although most statues remain unsigned, some came from Germany. St. Louis' German-trained sculptor Max Schneider-hahn copyrighted "The Agony in the Garden" (1903). His son served as one of the St. Francis de Sales priests in 1900. German artist Fridolin Fuchs decorated the church in 1916. Mosaic work depicting St. Francis de Sales over the exterior entrance and installations in the baptistery apse probably date to around 1920 when mosaicists were at work in the New Cathedral (#56) on Lindell.

56. Cathedral of St. Louis CL, CHD "New Cathedral"
4431 Lindell Boulevard (at Newstead Avenue)
1907: Barnett, Haynes & Barnett, St. Louis

Plans to relocate St. Louis' Old Cathedral (#1) involved three successive archbishops. Early 1870s plans made by Archbishop Kenrick proved misguided since rapid city development soon extended far west of the lot he had

Cathedral of St. Louis construction, c. 1909. Star Photo Co. Missouri Historical Society.

Cathedral of St. Louis, construction workers, c. 1909. Star Photo Co. Missouri Historical Society.

Cathedral of St. Louis construction, interior, c. 1910. Missouri Historical Society.

Cathedral of St. Louis, c. 1954. St. Louis Public Library.

selected a few blocks from his adoptive cathedral, St. John's (#7). In 1896, Archbishop Kain revived the cathedral project, purchased the present Lindell Boulevard parcel, built a provisional chapel on a corner of the lot and directed Roman Catholic architects Barnett, Haynes & Barnett to draw up cathedral plans. Kain died while the Catholic community raised funds for this design, a large, domed basilica with two-story Classical portico recalling Renaissance Vatican Rome. His youthful successor, Coadjutor John Joseph Glennon (1862 - 1946), took up the cathedral project in 1905 but decided to solicit new design concepts.

Glennon devised a competition program that called for a million-dollar church. Firms who submitted plans included Von Ferbulis (Austria and Washington, D. C.); McGinnis, Walsh & Sullivan (Boston); J. De Mentureal (Paris); Rüdell & Odenthal (Cologne), architects for St. Louis' Holy Cross Church (#52); and Barnett, Haynes & Barnett, the only local firm to enter. The St. Louis Chapter of the American Institute of Architects had asked members to boycott in protest over the lack of prize money for competitors and insufficient compensation for the winner. A 1905 aside in *American Architect* suggested instead that the Chapter was irritated by Glennon's apparent lack of confidence in local architects, as evidenced by his competition invitation to "foreign" architects. After touring European cathedrals in late summer 1905, Glennon stated that his St. Louis church would combine Romanesque, Byzantine, and Renaissance styles. In February 1906, the Building Committee declared Barnett, Haynes

Cathedral of St. Louis, c. 1987. Landmarks collection.

& Barnett winners of the competition.

The firm's final Romanesque-Byzantine design owed something to London's Westminster Cathedral (1895 - 1903) which ventured into the Byzantine style as a Catholic alternative to nineteenth-century Anglican Gothic. Ground was broken May 1, 1907. When completed in 1914, the cathedral, seating "five or six thousand people" had cost more than $3.25 million. "New and original" reinforced concrete structural forms under-pinned an exterior of severe New Hampshire gray granite walls; mosaic decorations designed to be placed over windows and doors were never carried out. Although the imposing dome was covered with shiny green-glazed tiles, the somber exterior gave little hint of an interior that evokes St. Mark's in Venice.

Architect George I. Barnett envisioned a religious art palace. "Intended to be almost barbaric in the grandeur of its color," the interior shell received the first of some 83,000 square feet of mosaics in 1912: the two west chapels were designed in thirteenth-century Italian style by Aristide Leonari for Tiffany & Co. (New York). Mosaic work continued off and on for seven decades until completion in 1988. Ravenna Mosaic Co. installed most of the mosaics designed by various artists after 1923. Local art glass manufacturer Emil Frei and Paul Heuduck (associate of Berlin mosaicist August Wagner, Inc.) organized the firm. Bronze doors came from the Austrian Exhibit at the St. Louis World's Fair. Barnett designed the elaborate high altar baldachin and the northeast Blessed Sacrament chapel, executed 1916-17 by the Gorham Co. Artist Hildreth Meier (New York), who designed mosaics for Nebraska's capitol, worked on the south "Dome of Local History."

Barnett, Hayes and Barnett's church designs outside St. Louis include St. Clement's, Chicago (a modest spinoff of the New Cathedral), and cathedrals in Montevideo, Uruguay, and Porto Alege, Brazil.

57. Pleasant Green Missionary Baptist Church
Shaare Zedek
4570 Page Boulevard (at Reverend George Pruitt Place)
1913: Architect unknown

St. Louis orthodox Jewry displayed new status through architecture when construction began in 1913 for the first temple ever erected by a St. Louis orthodox congregation. Because tradition dictated that members walk to services, small neighborhood temples (often rented or adapted from other uses) became the rule. By contrast, Shaare Zedek's stylized Classicism celebrated contemporary fashion while its prominent semicircular gables revived distinguished nineteenth-century temple designs. Steel trusses supported a four-sided domical roof. Large lunettes, glazed with opalescent glass Star of David motifs in the centers, generously illuminated a central-plan auditorium with concrete curving balcony.

Shaare Zedek, c. 1924. Missouri Historical Society.

Geometric Art Nouveau ornament was sparingly employed. In 1924-25, Shaare Zedek completed a large brick and terra cotta Education Center, reportedly the first institution of Jewish learning built in St. Louis.

Part of a new wave of Eastern European immigrants entering the United States in the early twentieth century, a small group of Lithuanian Jews chartered the congregation of Shaare Zedek (Hebrew words meaning "Gates of Righteousness") on October 27, 1905. Unlike the economically strong and well-established German Reformed community exemplified by Temple Israel (#48), these Orthodox newcomers had small means and settled in a less affluent near north side corridor.

Shaare Zedek's congregation first rented a hall at Vandeventer and Finney. In 1907, they purchased a house located in the same block as the future temple and converted it to religious use. Proposals in 1913 and again in 1916 failed to merge Shaare Zedek and B'nai Amoona, by then the two largest and most prosperous Orthodox congregations in the city. Apparently, an issue of where women should sit blocked the merger. Shaare Zedek followed the standard Orthodox practice of placing women in an upper balcony; B'nai Amoona allowed both sexes on the same level but in separate sections.

During the World War II era, a new ethnic group replaced the old orthodox neighborhood which migrated further west. In 1952, Shaare Zedek moved into a new synagogue in St. Louis County. Pleasant Green Baptist, a black congregation established in 1866, purchased the synagogue in 1945. George H. Pruitt (1885 - 1978), their pastor of nearly four decades, received due recognition when a street in front of the church was renamed in his honor.

58. Pope St. Pius V Roman Catholic Church

3310 S. Grand Avenue (at Utah Street)
1916: J. Sidney Lee (Lee & Rush), St. Louis

Father John Lyons, born and ordained in Ireland, organized this parish in 1905 when the area was still thinly populated but poised for rapid development thanks to a network of streetcar lines. The parish was named for one of the Vatican's most important Counter Reformation popes, Pius V (1504-1572). The name also paid tribute to Pope Pius X, elected two years before the parish's founding. The 1916 announcement by the *St. Louis Republican* that this building would be a "model of the Romanesque style of architecture of the sixteenth century" also associated the St. Louis church with the period of Pope Pius V. The pontificate of Pius V (1566-72) saw the beginning of construction on the famous Roman church, Il Jesu. The designs of the two churches, in Rome and St. Louis, invite loose comparison. Both have a two-story Baroque facade faced with pilasters; both interiors have clerestoried broad arcaded naves (without side aisles) covered with monumental barrel-vaulted ceilings.

Built at a cost of $250,000, the church exhibits fine Carthage stone masonry that effectively contrasts with a Spanish red tile roof. The *St. Louis Republican* reported that installation of marble altars would be delayed until after World War I, "when the skilled artisans in that line of work will have returned to their studios." Enrichment of the semi-circular apse finally came in 1937 with a $50,000 mosaic depicting "Christ as King Receiving Homage." The tower was originally designed for electric chimes because of neighborhood objection to bells. When bells were eventually installed in 1940, the tower required strengthening with steel beams to carry the weight. Vibrations from the bells necessitated further tower alterations in the late 1950s. The discovery of other structural flaws led to the replacement of window tracery with aluminum frames.

Pius V's life is celebrated in a schematic 1950s bas-relief above the entrance that refers to the Pope's institution of the feast of the Holy Rosary and his struggle to stem the tide of Islam. Structural problems required the removal of two elaborate sculptural groups by Victor Holm, Washington University Professor of Art. Originally part of the church facade, the groupings are shown in the photo (see page 98). The gable group portrayed the pontiff's 1571

Pope St. Pius V Roman Catholic Church, 1917. Photo: Frank M. White. Mercantile Library.

floor gymnasium enlarged the school in 1925. Facing Grand Avenue, a stone rectory built in 1958 replaced a 1909 priests' house destroyed by fire.

59. St. Roch's Roman Catholic Church CHD

6052 Waterman Boulevard (at Rosedale Avenue) 1921: Lee & Rush, St. Louis

An exuberant display of ornamental white terra cotta on St. Roch's brick walls is testimony to the parish's proud achievement within the short span of a decade after its founding. (The design, however, was not without critics. Church historian Reverend John Rothensteiner suggested in 1928 that the building's rich ornamentation went "really beyond the limit of good taste.") A restricted church lot demanded an efficient plan allowing no wasted space for interior columns or aisles; space was also conserved by a feature hailed as "novel" in which the choir loft and organ were placed on either side of the main altar. Described at the time as "Tudor Gothic," the church became the crowning piece in an integrated ensemble that included a 1912 school and 1915 rectory.

triumph over Turkish infidels after the Battle of Lepanto. A crucifixion scene filled the arch of the entrance tympanum.

Behind today's church, a 1906 stone school and former chapel by Joseph Stauder (St. Louis) serve as reminders of the parish's phenomenal growth over the course of twelve years, from about fifty families to over 700 in 1917. A third-

St. Roch's. **Photo: Robert C. Pettus, 1995.** *Landmarks Association.*

The founding of St. Roch's in a small neighborhood store in 1911 was the result of a tremendous building boom after the 1904 World's Fair. The new parish boundaries crossed city limits to the west where Parkview Place (opened in 1905) had already attracted faculty members from Washington University. The developing row of mansions in the Catlin Tract facing Forest Park on Lindell Boulevard also belonged to St. Roch's parish. It was the eastern boundary that was a sore point: prestigious Washington Terrace and Kingsbury Place were reserved for the Cathedral parish.

According to a parish history, St. Roch's owes its name to the highest bidder at a church fund-raiser arranged by a resourceful pastor, Father Kuhlman. A dedication sermon in 1922 referred to the aptness of naming a church after a layman, a distinction the parish continued to acknowledge in later years while admitting that their knowledge of St. Roch remained slim. A fourteenth-century saint born in Montpelier, France, St. Roch never belonged to a religious order. His cult as patron of the plague-stricken spread through western Europe; it revived during nineteenth-century cholera epidemics.

60. Bostick Temple Church of God in Christ
West Park Baptist Church
5988 Wells Avenue (at Hodiamont Avenue)
1925: Hoener, Baum & Froese, St. Louis

Allusion to Early Christian building types (notably octagonal baptisteries) was a felicitous choice for the design of a Baptist church. For West Park Baptist, architects Hoener, Baum & Froese combined a distinctive octagonal form with artful brick and terra cotta work to create a small Arts & Crafts gem both inside and out. Lombard Romanesque-style brickwork in variegated buff and brown was subtly accented with Winkle Terra Cotta Co. blocks at the cornice and around openings. Interior ornamentation of exposed glazed brick, textured plaster, and mosaic banding emphasized materials. A simple wood truss ceiling with beams radiating from a center point underscored the polygonal centralized plan. Windows were glazed with pastel-color leaded glass set in a diamond pattern. A baptismal pool behind the chancel arch served as the focal point of the auditorium. The organ console (now removed) was subordinated to a pit, its pipes concealed behind screens.

West Park Baptist began as a Sabbath School in 1893, when some members of Third Baptist Church on Grand Avenue, led by realtor William B. Harris, relocated to a small frame building at Morton and Chatham in what is now Wellston. In 1901, the congregation moved east into the city where they erected a modest brick building in the 5900 block of Easton Avenue. West Park Baptist became an independent church in 1904, and Third Baptist

West Park Baptist, c. 1926. Hoener & Associates.

West Park Baptist, c. 1926. Hoener & Associates.

transferred memberships. As the congregation continued to grow, members began planning for a larger church. World War I Liberty Bonds and War Stamps bolstered the building fund. After the war, the present site was purchased for $11,890 in 1923. Ground was broken in 1925. The 540-seat, $150,000 church included a sizable annex housing Sunday school, social and office rooms. In 1960, the West Park congregation voted to relocate in St. Louis county where more than half of its members lived.

Bostick Temple, the city's oldest congregation of the Church of God in Christ, moved into the church at 5988 Wells in 1962. Daniel Bostick founded the congregation in 1908 after withdrawing from the A.M.E. church. A series of westward moves (beginning at Eleventh and Cole) stopped in 1913 with a church at Twenty-

third and Delmar where membership swelled to more than 800. For many years the congregation observed an annual tradition of baptism in the Mississippi River. Changes in the neighborhood brought them to the present site.

61. St. Ambrose Roman Catholic Church
5130 Wilson Avenue (at Marconi Avenue)
1925: Angelo Corrubia, St. Louis

The claim "handmade in Italy" comes close to describing the collaborative effort of the St. Louis Italians who built this Catholic church in the neighborhood popularly known as The Hill. Clay dug from nearby pits was fashioned by Italian laborers, artisans, craftsmen, and architect Angelo

St. Ambrose, 1989. Photo: W. Philip Cotton, Jr. AIA St. Louis.

St. Ambrose, c. 1947. Archdiocesan Archives.

Corrubia into a building that expressed a close alliance of nationalism and religion. (The community's Northern Lombard roots prevailed in the church design despite an attempt to balance factious northern Lombard and southern Sicilian members of the Building Committee.) *Globe-Democrat* coverage of the cornerstone-laying on May 30, 1925 attributed inspiration of the design to "the beautiful churches of Lombardy, as for example, St. Ambrogio, Milan; St. Petronio, Bologna; and St. Maria delle Grazie, Milan. The brick is shale brick, resembling very closely the brick of the old churches of this style." The national popularity of Lombard Romanesque for Catholic churches at this time no doubt also influenced architect Angelo Corrubia, a native of Italy trained at Washington University (St. Louis) and M.I.T.

"The Italian Immigrants," 1995. Photo: Landmarks Association, Cynthia Hill Longwisch.

A veritable St. Louis "Who's Who" of the Italian building arts can be found in the names of firms that worked on St. Ambrose. Most of the principals had emigrated around the turn of the century. Some brought unique skills such as Raphael Paolinelli's ornamental scagliola work (plasterwork imitating marble), in demand throughout Missouri. Others represented St. Louis' Italian-controlled marble and terrazzo industry. Calogero Rallo and Ignazio Brugnone, Sicilian partners of the construction company, commanded a prosperous local business in the 1920s which grew into one of the Midwest's largest. While not of Italian extraction, the owners of St. Louis Terra Cotta and Hydraulic Brick were major employers of Italians from The Hill who fabricated St. Ambrose's brick and ornamental terra cotta.

Father Spigardi of St. Charles Borromeo (#12) organized St. Ambrose in 1903. In the late nineteenth century, work opportunities in clay mines and brickyards of the Fairmount Heights district (long known as Cheltenham) attracted the earliest wave of Italian immigrants to the area. Through chain migration, this nucleus of male laborers evolved into an unusually stable, prosperous working-class community which survives to the present day. A poignant bronze statue, "The Italian Immigrants" (1972), at the northwest corner of the church, is the work of St. Louis sculptor Rudolph Torrini.

THE SKINKER BOULEVARD GROUP

The last frontier of the westward march from city to county, Skinker Boulevard attracted three congregations in the 1920s to its green-edged blocks bordering Forest Park. A fourth church arrived in 1951. The first to break ground and the oldest congregation, United Hebrew began construction in 1924. Previously, they occupied what had been a Christian church (razed) at N. Kingshighway and Enright, a few blocks north of the eastern boundary of Forest Park and two blocks away from Temple Israel (#48). Memorial

Presbyterian, under construction in 1925, traveled the longest distance--from Washington and Compton Avenues, where the congregation had worshipped in a church they built in 1877 (#19). Eighth Church of Christ, Scientist came the shortest distance, arriving on Wydown in 1928 from Waterman and DeBaliviere Avenues. Finally, Central Church of Christ left Euclid and Cote Brilliante for a 1951 red brick Gothic Revival building by Gale E. Henderson at 305 South Skinker.

62. Memorial Presbyterian Church NRD
201 S. Skinker Boulevard (at Alexander Drive)
1925: Albert B. Groves, St. Louis
1931: Aegerter & Bailey

A Gothic Revival-style, 85-foot-high stone bell tower and chapel by Albert B. Groves announced the arrival of Memorial Presbyterian in 1926. By the end of 1931, the congregation completed the church with a seven-bay auditorium that exploited an oblique siting on the wedge-shaped lot. St. Louis craftsmen and building suppliers included Pickel Stone Co. for the cut stone, Davis Art Glass Co. for art glass windows, LeCoutour Bros. Stair Manufacturing Co. for interior millwork, and St. Louis Steel Erection Co. for the structural steel work. All were specially recognized at the dedication ceremony. The principal entrance features a large Perpendicular Gothic-styled window framed by pinnacled buttressing. The near-original interior survives with carved dark oak pulpit, lectern, baptismal font, pews (by American Seating Co., Chicago), and hanging lamps of brass and glass (Gross Chandelier, St. Louis). A tie-beam truss system articulates the ceiling.

During its earlier history, the congregation followed a fairly common Protestant practice of choosing street names for the title of the church. Whenever a congregation moved to a new location, church names changed accordingly. Organized in 1864 as a dissident offshoot of Second Presbyterian (#43), the new group first called itself the Sixteenth Street or Walnut Street Church, then changed its name

Memorial Presbyterian. **Photo: Robert C. Pettus, 1989.** *Landmarks Association.*

to Washington & Compton Avenue Presbyterian (#19) in the late 1870s after it moved to Midtown. The present name, Memorial Presbyterian, became official after a vote in 1926.

63. Eighth Church of Christ, Scientist NRD

6221 Alexander Drive (at Wydown Avenue)
1928: Aegerter & Bailey, St. Louis

Deviating from the Classical standard found in other St. Louis Christian Science churches, Aegerter & Bailey introduced in Eighth Church a decorative North Italian Gothic design which they employed again across town in Seventh Church (1930). Both buildings display a rich variety of ornamental brickwork with terra cotta detailing; they also share similar polygonal central plans. In keeping with Christian

Eighth Church of Christ, Scientist, 1995. Photo: Landmarks Association, Cynthia Hill Longwisch.

Science tradition, interiors of both churches were handled with great restraint. Seventh Church (now New Testament Christian Church) features an austere modernistic Classicism designed by Chicago architect Charles Faulkner, a Christian Scientist. Eighth Church's subdued auditorium follows Christian Science conventions with theater-style, fan-shaped seating focusing on the reader's desk.

The plan, however, diverges from the usual Christian Science type by placement of the 1,000-seat auditorium on the same level as the entry foyer rather than on an upper story. The building's exceptionally large two-story foyer originally was intended to serve as the church proper; however, a spring discovered on the site caused foundation problems, necessitating a change in plan. (During the 1904 World's Fair, the U.S. Life Saving Lake occupied the present wedge-shaped lot.) Eighth Church subsequently purchased an adjoining west lot where the auditorium was built.

Overflow attendance at Fourth Church of Christ, Scientist (Page Boulevard) brought about the organization of Eighth Church in 1926. The congregation held services in Dorr & Zeller Hall (Waterman and DeBaliviere) until completion of the east foyer-Sunday school unit in 1929.

64. Missouri Historical Society Archives NRD
United Hebrew Congregational Temple
225 S. Skinker Boulevard
1924: Maritz & Young with Gabriel Ferrand, St. Louis

United Hebrew was the first Jewish congregation established west of the Mississippi. Organized in 1837, the congregation began as Orthodox, then gradually evolved to Reform ritual by adopting practices such as the use of a choir, an organ, and finally, in 1913, the Union Prayer Book. At the time of the temple de-

Drawing: United Hebrew Congregational Temple, c. 1924. St. Louis Public Library.

dication in 1927, United Hebrew's 650-family membership
made it the largest Jewish
group in the city. The new
temple was the fifth building
they occupied and the third
they constructed. (The first
four have been razed.) Plan,
not style, was the primary design problem for the architects
who had to meet the chal-
lenging demands for seating
on major Jewish holidays
when "every member of the
Congregation feels it to be a
religious duty to come to the
Synagogue." Those occasions
required capacity to be nearly
doubled. The architects
increased seating by 750
through the introduction of
large "convertible" side wings
screened off from the auditorium by velvet curtains.
Total capacity, including
balconies, could reach 2,200.

The dramatic auditorium,
now successfully preserved as
the library reading room of the
Missouri Historical Society,
exhibits elaborate ornamental
plasterwork in the dome executed by architectural sculptor Victor Berlendis. Floral
motifs are combined with traditional non-figural Jewish
symbols.

Immanuel Lutheran Church. **Photo: Robert C. Pettus, 1995.** *Landmarks Association.*

United Hebrew Temple, reportedly one of
the three largest Jewish synagogues in the
nation, was built for $750,000 from plans by
Maritz & Young (St. Louis) with consulting
architect Gabriel Ferrand. Then head of
Washington University's School of
Architecture, French-born Ferrand (1876-1934)
attributed his inspiration for the 82-foot-
diameter dome to that of Hagia Sophia in
Istanbul. The overall style for the Temple
acknowledged historic Middle Eastern origins,
but interpreted the past with a new emphasis
on compact, simple geometric volumes and

direct, artistic expression of materials. The
Temple was converted for use by the Missouri
Historical Society in 1992 following plans by
Ted Wofford (St. Louis), whose firm also
designed an unassuming addition.

65. Immanuel Lutheran Church

3530 Marcus Avenue (at Lexington Avenue)
1927: Ewald Froese (Hoener, Baum &
Froese), St. Louis

Immanuel Lutheran Church originated in 1844

Immanuel Lutheran Church. **Photo: Robert C. Pettus, 1995.**
Landmarks Association.

Among the graves of some 2,000 Lutherans is that of Pastor J. F. Buenger.

Funds to begin a new church were provided by the International Shoe Company's purchase of the old Delmar church property in 1925. Two years later, Immanuel member Ewald Froese drew up plans. The cornerstone laid in 1927 held the entire contents of the old Delmar church cornerstone including Reverend Buenger's declaration (in German) of the early leaders' strong faith: "Rather than to see Rationalism, religious fanaticism, false Lutheranism preached in this church, the builders would that God destroy the building by fire, storm, or an earthquake." Froese's clerestory design with low side aisles "in the style of the English country church" features a heavy timber ceiling. A massive tower housing the entry vestibule dominates the exterior. The belfry contains bells cast in 1880 for Immanuel's Delmar Street church. Surprisingly in a city known for its brickmakers, brick for the church was supplied by Dalton Bros. of Hopkinsville, Kentucky.

Born in Danzig, Poland, architect Ewald Froese (1888 - 1958) took exceptional care in designing his own church. Keen interest in all branches of liturgical art, including music, led him personally to design chancel paraments and to detail wood carvings and ornament. North side cabinetmaker Ferdinand Maguola (president of Century Woodworking) executed Froese's designs for the altar, pews, pulpit, lectern, and *pre dieu*. The altar oil painting, "Christ Immanuel" by Brooklyn artist R. Scheffler, derived from Froese's sketches of a European icon. Emil Frei Studios (St. Louis) supplied the art glass windows and a mosaic above the front door.

as a school mission at Seventh and Cole Streets on the city's near north side. Construction began on a church at Eleventh and Franklin (now Dr. Martin Luther King Drive) Streets within three years. The second Lutheran congregation in St. Louis, Immanuel was led by Reverend J. F. Buenger who was among the earliest German Saxon immigrants. That group formed Missouri's first Lutheran Church, Trinity (#41), in the Soulard neighborhood. During the early years, Buenger and Trinity's Reverend C. F. W. Walther alternately conducted services at each church. Walther, the patriarch of Missouri Synod Lutherans, made Immanuel the Second District Church of the four he controlled until his death in 1887.

In 1868, Immanuel relocated to a new church and adjoining school at Fifteenth and Delmar where the congregation remained for nearly fifty years. The third and final move was not made until 1919 when the congregation took a giant leap to a far northwest section of the city. A temporary brick chapel was erected on the grounds of the Western Lutheran Cemetery. Laid out in 1863, the cemetery remains adjacent to the present church site.

66. Our Lady of Sorrows Roman Catholic Church
5831 S. Kingshighway Boulevard (at Rhodes Avenue)
1927: Adolph F. Stauder, St. Louis

Anti-Catholic sentiment delayed Our Lady's first attempts to purchase land for a church. Acquisition in 1909 of this three-acre site surrounded by ponds, truck gardens, and a cemetery required the help of a straw party. In the early years, the parish comprised both English- and German-speaking members. Names of subdivisions opened in 1906 (Austria, Humboldt, Beethoven, Hannover, and Hildesheim Heights) appealed to St. Louis German-Americans. Five new parishes on the growing south side were carved out of Our Lady of Sorrows' territory between 1914 and 1919.

A 1911 school facing S. Kingshighway became the first building on the present site. (The school received a new brick and terra cotta facade in 1952.) Two parishioners, Adolph and Arthur Stauder (father and son) designed all of the buildings in the church complex. Founded circa 1870 by builder-architect Joseph Stauder (Adolph's father), the firm became prominent builders of Catholic institutions in the Midwest. St. Louis church designs by Adolph and Arthur include St. Mary Magdalen (1940), South Side Unity Church (1941), and St. Gabriel the Archangel Catholic Church (1950) (#76).

The design of the new church completed in 1928 recalls the Basilica of St. Paul's Outside the Walls in Rome. Both exhibit colonnaded porches and interior flat coffered ceilings above colonnaded naves. Historian John Rothensteiner noted in 1928 that two design features – the columned portico and placement of the campanile in front of the transept – represented "an innovation in Catholic church design in St. Louis." Walls of brick provided by St. Louis Hydraulic Brick were laid by a south side firm, Niehaus & Eckerich, over a steel frame skeleton provided by Banner Iron Co. (St. Louis). Decorative brickwork and a tall campanile evoke North Italian Lombard style.

In 1938, the church's interior furnishings and decoration were completed. Schiller & Associates (St. Louis) painted life-size stations

Our Lady of Sorrows, 1995. Photo: Landmarks Association: Carolyn Hewes Toft.

Our Lady of Sorrows, 1995. Landmarks Association: Carolyn Hewes Toft.

of the cross; Schiller associate Joseph Schrader provided marble side altars and a main altar with bronze canopy. The Emil Frei Co. (St. Louis) installed stained glass windows. Although the original design called for a mosaic dome over the altar along with mosaic stations of the cross, neither were carried out. In 1957, gold imitation mosaic refurbished a 1938 dome painting.

67. St. James the Greater Roman Catholic Church
1345 Tamm Avenue (at Wade Avenue)
1927: O'Meara & Hills, St. Louis

"You have in this temple the best that craftsmanship can accomplish in wood, stone, bronze, iron, plaster and furniture . . . . I would like to make this church the Cathedral of the South Side." This tribute, delivered by Archbishop Glennon at its dedication in 1928, celebrated the Arts & Crafts achievement embodied in St. James' rich display of the allied arts. Formerly of St. Paul, Minnesota, architects Patrick M. O'Meara and James B. Hills

(prominent architects of Midwestern Catholic institutions) opened a St. Louis office in 1923. O'Meara and Hills grounded their practice in a gospel of Arts & Crafts theory that stressed, above all, the importance of all the arts to architecture. A corollary ideal called for collaboration between craftsman and designer as joint authors. The firm worked closely with Minneapolis artist Thomas J. Gaytee on this church as well as on St. Wenceslaus Church and other St. Louis projects.

Gaytee designed most interior furnishings and decorations. Stained glass windows, tapestry paintings, stations of the cross, crucifixes, sanctuary lights, tabernacles, and candlesticks were all fruits of his concepts. (Donors of stained glass windows included O'Meara & Hills and Gaytee.) Arts & Crafts insistence on "honest" materials and its preference for an imperfect finish were evidenced in St. James' hammered metal, natural finish wormy chestnut (used extensively in an open truss ceiling), organ case, and other areas. Stained, mottled limestone and irregular-surfaced Mankato rock were selected for the altar.

Understated handling of the Bedford limestone design won special approval from St. James' Father Patrick J. O'Connor whose four decades of parish service (1912 - 1952) continued an unbroken line of Irish-born priests. Craftsman philosophy became adroitly linked to ethnic heritage when Father O'Connor explained that the church reflected "craftsmanship as done in Ireland," adding that its "eleventh-century Gothic" style represented a period in Ireland which valued fine craft objects above the perfection of architectural form characteristic in other periods. St. James' Irish legacy continues to be honored today with St. Patrick's Day celebrations featuring Hibernian parades, special masses, Irish food, music, and dance.

Detail: St. James the Greater, 1995. Photo: Landmarks Association, Carolyn Hewes Toft.

Cheltenham. Descendants of the Gratiot family were still active parishioners as well as donors to the new church in 1927.

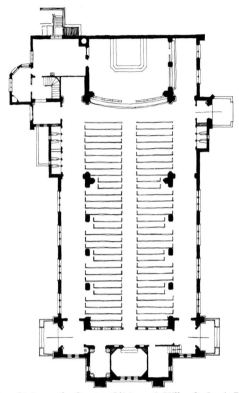

Plan: St. James the Greater. O'Meara & Hills. St. Louis Public Library.

A mission of St. Malachy at Clark and Ewing, St. James opened in 1861 to serve industrial workers in the suburb of Cheltenham (absorbed by the expansion of the St. Louis city limits in 1876). St. Louis Smelting & Refining Co., along with several brick, clay- and coal-mining companies, attracted Irish, Welsh, and German immigrants. Within a year, the congregation erected a church on the opposite side of Tamm from the present church. The land was donated by Henry T. Gratiot, descendent of a French family whose 8,000-acre Spanish Land Grant (the Gratiot League) included

St. James the Greater, 1927. St. Louis Public Library.

68. St. Michael the Archangel Russian Orthodox Church NRD

1901 Ann Avenue
1928: Charles L. Thurston (city unknown)

Orthodox mission churches in America faced new political realities following the 1917 Bolshevik Revolution. Severed from the Russian mother church, previously a means of support, struggling congregations took stock of their resources. When St. Louis building inspectors condemned St. Michael's makeshift church (a converted residence at 1125 Hickory), the shrewd pastor booked the Russian Rite Church Choir for a local benefit tour. The tour elicited rave reviews and engaged prominent sponsors. Former Mayor Henry Kiel and the President of the Board of Aldermen headed a committee to raise funds to buy a lot and construct a church. The building was dedicated in 1929. Although modest in size, the brown brick Byzantine-style church evoked the congregation's exotic Eastern heritage. Its green-tiled principal dome was echoed in small onion-domed turrets. A sparsely decorated exterior together with a compact central plan and traditional icons inside also followed Orthodox design conventions.

Russian immigration to St. Louis increased significantly between 1890 and 1910, leaping from about 1,500 to over 15,000. Not all professed the Orthodox faith. Industrial jobs drew Russians to the city, many from earlier settlements in the mining area of Desloge, Missouri. St. Michael's Church was formed in 1909; the Hickory Street house was converted to religious use the next year. A fund drive brochure from 1926 expressed the immigrant values of the 95-family congregation which, it was said, proudly upheld the "best traditions of the melting pot," and stood "as a rock against Bolshevism and its attendant evils." Members boasted citizenship, literacy in English, children enrolled in public schools, and loyalty to the religion of Mother Russia.

St. Michael the Archangel, c. 1928. St. Louis Public Library.

69. Scruggs Memorial United Methodist Church

3443 Grace Avenue (at Fairview Avenue)
1929: Ferrand & Fitch, St. Louis

In 1930, Scruggs Methodist Church was hailed by contemporary journalists as the first church in St. Louis to be designed in the "American Colonial style." However, it remained one of the few examples ever built in the city. Many congregations held deep-seated beliefs that Gothic was the only proper style for churches and that Colonial Revival was a style better suited for secular buildings such as banks, schools, and houses. To supporters of the style, Colonial Revival was

Scruggs Memorial United Methodist. Ferrand & Fitch, 1929. Mercantile Library.

sanctified by its venerable roots in early American history and heroes. The style inspired patriotic feelings and fostered convictions that Colonial Revival was the only truly "American" style. In the St. Louis region, Colonial Revival church design became popular in the developing suburbs.

Funds to build this church came in part from the sale of an older Methodist house of worship on Cook Avenue (#23) which department store founder and church benefactor Richard M. Scruggs (1822 -1904) had heavily endowed. To preserve Scruggs' legacy, the Methodist Quarterly Conference stipulated that any new church built with funds from the Cook Avenue church must carry the name of Richard M. Scruggs. The Church Extension Society selected the Grand Avenue Methodist congregation, then in need of a larger building, as beneficiary.

Grand Avenue Methodist was founded in 1905 at Grand and Connecticut Avenues. Brothers Richard M. and C. O. Scruggs gave financial support to the new congregation; C. O. Scruggs organized and superintended

the Sunday school. By the late 1920s, the disruptive noise of heavy traffic on Grand Avenue led the congregation to seek a quieter location for a new church. The *St. Louis Globe-Democrat* reported in 1929 that the removal of the Methodist church from Grand Avenue to Grace and Fairview "illustrates the remarkable commercial activity which has come to this district. A price of $95,000 has been paid for the corner by a real estate firm which will erect an apartment house thereon."

Architects Gabriel Ferrand and Austin E. Fitch formed a partnership in 1918 when both men held faculty positions in Washington University's School of Architecture. Ferrand was head of the School and professor of design; Fitch was a professor of architectural construction. Born in Toulouse, France, Ferrand studied architecture at the *Ecole des Beaux Arts* in Toulouse and Paris. In 1931, the President of France named Ferrand a *Chevalier* of the Legion of Honor, France's highest honor. Fitch graduated from Washington University's School of Architecture, then earned a master's degree from Harvard in 1916. During the 1940s he served as Assistant Dean of Washington University's School of Engineering. His interest in the structural aspects of design is evident in an engineering feature of Scruggs Church which provided a large basement room without supporting pillars. Ferrand's scholarly design expertise is evident in the Colonial Revival detailing of the church.

70. All Saints' Episcopal Church (Faith German Evangelical Lutheran Church)

2821 N. Kingshighway Boulevard (at Terry Avenue)
1930: Aegerter & Bailey, St. Louis

Faith Lutheran's congregation began construction of this red brick church four years after its organization in 1926. An offshoot of Grace Lutheran, Faith belonged to the United Lutheran Church of America. The Tudor Gothic design executed at a cost of $235,000 represented the latest fashion of Gothic Revival substyles. The principal entrance was placed on N. Kingshighway; a secondary tower entrance faces Terry Street where, at the west end of the nave, a two-story parish building is attached. Articulation of the near-original interior recalls Aegerter & Bailey's handling of Memorial Presbyterian (#62). Both employed distinctive wood tie-beam truss ceilings. Faith's ceiling introduced decoratively patterned acoustic tile, a progressive feature at the time.

The interior plan follows a traditional rectangular shape with the center aisle flanked by straight rows of pews. Noteworthy carved wood liturgical art includes a large crucifixion figural group in the south chapel and an

All Saints' Episcopal, 1995. Photo: Landmarks Association, Cynthia Hill Longwisch.

elaborate filigree Gothic reredos crowned with figures of the Evangelists. Big nave windows (nearly floor to ceiling) display opalescent art glass punctuated in the center with small Christian symbols. Floral and geometric patterns form borders and fill tracery.

In 1957, Faith moved west into St. Louis county and sold the church to All Saints' Episcopal Church, Missouri's first and only African-American parish according to Charles Rehkopf, archivist for the diocese. All Saints' organized in 1874 as the Mission of Our Savior Sunday School. The group acquired its first building the next year (the former B'nai El Synagogue at Sixth and Cerre; razed) and adopted the name Good Shepherd. In 1881, the mission relocated nearer the black community in shared space at Trinity Episcopal church at Eleventh and Washington. Good Shepherd gained full parish status in 1883. The diocese conferred the name All Saints' Episcopal Church and the new parish moved west to Twenty-second and Washington into the former Central Christian Church building. Another westward move in 1906 found the congregation at Locust and Garrison where All Saints' took possession of an impressive 1879 church (razed) designed by Peabody & Stearns (Boston) for the Unitarian Church of the Messiah (see #51). The Episcopalians purchased the Garrison Street church for $35,000; they received $50,000 for the Washington Avenue property, a prime development site in the garment district.

All Saints' remained on Garrison for fifty years. When a survey revealed that all of the constituency now lived west of the church, the parish took steps to relocate to their present address. Today the influential, 500-member congregation draws largely from outlying areas, but All Saints' ministers to the immediate neighborhood as sponsor of an Adult Literacy Council, a food pantry, and scout troops.

71. Mount Olive Lutheran Church CHD
4246 Shaw Boulevard
1931: Theodore Steinmeyer, St. Louis

A square, Romanesque bell tower with modernistic setbacks provides a striking

Mount Olive Lutheran. **Photo: Robert C. Pettus, 1995.** *Landmarks Association.*

114

neighborhood landmark that distinguishes the church from surrounding buildings in the Shaw Historic District. On top of the tower's domed lantern, a stainless steel cross and terra cotta crown offer symbolic references to the Mount of Olives. The use of a round-arched Romanesque style ran contrary to the traditional Lutheran allegiance to Gothic, stirring controversy within the church hierarchy when photographs were first viewed in 1932. In support, Lutheran architectural critic and advisor Frederick R. Webber praised the simplicity and "fine effect" of Mt. Olive's interior, which, he claimed, improved upon "our business-like, assembly-room type of churches . . . of the last decade or so." An Arts & Crafts advocate, Webber also commended Mt. Olive's well-crafted ceiling which exhibited "trusses of honest timbers honestly joined together."

A rented store at 1816 Klemm served as the first house of worship in 1924 for Mount Olive Lutheran, which was organized as Shaw Mission under the auspices of Christ Lutheran Church. Two years later, the mission adopted the name Mount Olive Lutheran and converted a three-story residence on the present site into an all-purpose church, Sunday school, and parsonage. In 1928, Mount Olive incorporated and became a member of the Lutheran Church Missouri Synod. Plans prepared by Lutheran architect Theodore Steinmeyer (baptized in Holy Cross Church, #14) were accepted in April 1931, only five years after the congregation's founding.

Mt. Pleasant Missionary Baptist, 1995. Photo: Landmarks Association, Cynthia Hill Longwisch.

72. Mt. Pleasant Missionary Baptist Church

Lutheran Church of Our Savior
2854-58 Abner Place (at St. Louis Avenue)
1931: Theodore Steinmeyer

Favorable Depression prices helped this church obtain unusually low construction bids in 1932. Architect Theodore Steinmeyer, a leading Lutheran proponent of Arts & Crafts design, met budget by judiciously combining "modest materials, yet the best of their kind" with Early English Gothic, a style, he noted, which emphasized "ruggedness and unaffectedness, simplicity of materials and lines." Warm red and brown variegated brick supplied by Richards Brick Co. was laid by Uthoff & Strathmann; Wabash Stone Co. provided stone masonry trim. Purple and green slate from Lloyd Roofing Co. covered the roof.

The program of interior furnishing carefully planned by the architect was exhibited in a wood truss ceiling and carved chancel paneling. Steel nave windows set in stone displayed biblical figural medallions. Characteristic of Lutheran church design, the chancel window (tripart lancets) symbolized the Trinity. A copper flèche or spire set on the roof ridge served the practical function of ventilating the nave ceiling while adding visual interest to the design.

Church of Our Savior opened in 1916 as a mission in a small store at 5577 St. Louis Avenue, a couple of blocks west of the present church site. The next year the Lutherans acquired another store at 5404 St. Louis Avenue which they adapted for worship and used for six years. After purchasing the present site in 1921, the congregation completed the basement in 1923 where they worshipped until the church was finished in 1933.

73. St. Simon Cyrene
(St. Philip Neri Roman Catholic Church)
5076 Durant Avenue (at Thekla Street)
1931: Preston J. Bradshaw, St. Louis

Named for a sixteenth-century Italian saint and founder of the Oratorian Order, St. Philip Neri Church is also indebted to Italy for its architectural style. Tiers of arches articulating the facade recall Italian Romanesque churches as does the characteristic tall, detached bell tower or campanile. The $315,000 church built of smooth variegated red brick is trimmed with symbolic stone carvings illustrating "cardinal elements of Catholic theology," according to the April 5, 1931 *Globe-Democrat.* A statue of the church's namesake stands above the door.

Planned without conventional columns and side aisles, the interior is richly finished in Italian marble of several colors. Pulpit, baldachin altar, and baptismal font are also of marble variously accented with mosaics and marble inlays. Guidicy Marble Co. (St. Louis) furnished the marblework and decorative terrazzo floors. Mosaic stations of the cross are by Alsatian artist Martin Feuerstein. Stained glass windows (predominantly red and blue) came from the Munich studio of Emil Frei. An open timber ceiling incorporated acoustic tile

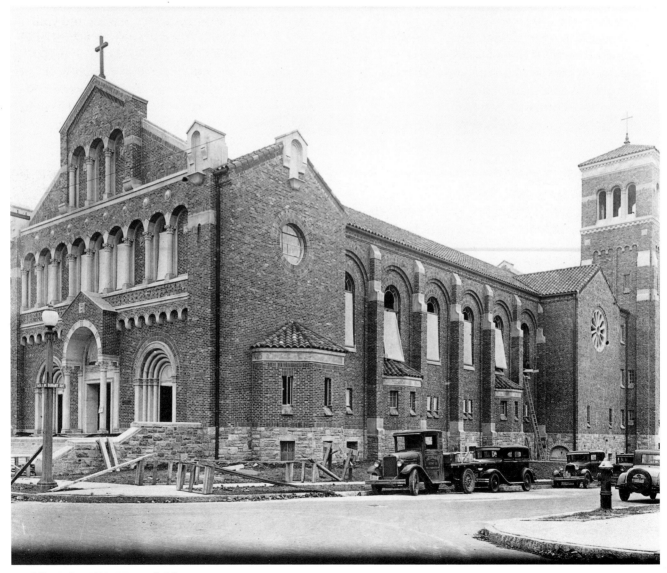

St. Philip Neri, c. 1931. Mercantile Library.

soffits. Contemporary descriptions indicate that architect Preston J. Bradshaw designed or directed nearly all of the original church furnishings and decoration.

St. Philip Neri parish opened in 1919 in Walnut Park, an emerging industrial district of northwest St. Louis. Recently returned from service in France during World War I, Reverend Thomas D. Kennedy, Chaplain of the 138th (St. Louis) Regiment, first held mass in a warehouse near the present church. Construction of a combination church-school began in 1921, the first building of several parish properties designed by Preston J. Bradshaw (1880-1949). A 1993 merger of St. Adalbert and St. Philip Neri parishes resulted in the current name, St. Simon Cyrene. A former sisters' convent (built the same year as the church) now serves as a women's center. A joint church and state program for teens, Caring Communities, is conducted in the old church-school building.

Bradshaw, a Roman Catholic born in St. Louis, received unusual recognition on the cornerstone inscription which carries only the architect's name. Bradshaw graduated from Columbia University and worked with Stanford White (New York) before returning to St. Louis. He enjoyed a successful practice specializing in commercial property, particularly large apartment buildings and hotels in which he sometimes held financial interest. St. Philip Neri is his only known church design.

74. St. Nicholas Greek Orthodox Church
4967 Forest Park Avenue
1930: E. K. Eugene, Chicago

A 1917 press caption--"Church Founded in Two Weeks, 150 Greeks Buy Edifice and Call Priest"-- in the *St. Louis Republican* (October 27, 1917) announced the new St. Nicholas parish and its purchase of an existing church building (formerly Grace Lutheran) at Garrison and St. Louis Avenue. Origins of Greek Orthodoxy in St. Louis, however, date from 1904 when a

St. Nicholas Greek Orthodox. **Photo: Robert C. Pettus, 1995.** *Landmarks Association.*

St. Nicholas Greek Orthodox. **Photo: Robert C. Pettus, 1995.** *Landmarks Association.*

small Greek colony (predominantly male) established Holy Trinity Church in a rented building at Nineteenth and Morgan (now Delmar). Monthly visits from Chicago clergy accommodated the congregation until it gained a permanent priest in 1906. (A second Greek parish, Annunciation, organized by a splinter group in 1910, dissolved in 1913.)

By 1916, St. Louis' growing Greek settlement, estimated at 5,000, owned more than 400 small businesses, including several movie houses and a large number of West End restaurants. Organization of St. Nicholas in 1917 (in truth, a restructured Holy Trinity) achieved significant unification of differing church factions. Solidarity was affirmed in 1918 when the Archbishop of the Church of Greece visited St. Louis as part of a World War I diplomatic mission to meet with U.S. President Wilson. The event helped the Greek

community gain new status in the civic life of St. Louis.

Old World Orthodox customs gradually underwent modification during the early 1920s. Nave chairs replaced a tradition of standing; women, formerly confined to balcony seating, joined men on the main floor. After a brief experiment in 1928 in which western-style church music met strong opposition, a more traditional Orthodox *a cappella* choir permanently replaced professional singers.

The 1927 tornado demolished St. Nicholas' church at Garrison and St. Louis Avenues. After renting a vacant synagogue at Kingshighway and Enright, the parish acquired a building site and hired Chicago architect Ernest K. Eugene to design its new home. Laying of the cornerstone took place on January 11, 1931, followed by the dedication on September 20, 1931. The modified

Romanesque Revival stone building reflected Eastern Orthodox design tradition: an austere, sparsely detailed exterior in contrast to a richly finished interior. In 1942, the congregation redecorated the church and installed a new bishop's throne, pulpit, and iconostasis. New stained glass windows from 1944-46 featuring figural panels in a distinctive geometric field greatly enhanced the nave.

Relocation of St. Nicholas came under discussion in the mid-1950s and again in 1959, when the congregation voted to remain in the city and enlarge its property. A community center addition designed by Raymond E. Maritz & Sons (St. Louis) dates from 1960.

75. St. Mark's Episcopal Church CL
4714 Clifton Avenue (at Murdoch Avenue)
1938: Nagel & Dunn, St. Louis

The design of St. Mark's pioneered new directions in St. Louis church design. Declared "a gem of modern architecture" in the January 21, 1939 edition of the *St. Louis Globe-Democrat*, the church was the result of a $75,000 bequest left by real estate dealer John A. Watkins. That sum covered land acquisition, design, construction, and handsome interior furnishings by local artists. Future expansion was carefully provided for in the original site plan by architects Nagel & Dunn. An addition to the church envisioning a cruciform plan was not built, but the rectory was added in 1950 followed by the parish house in 1955.

The tall, narrow building designed with simple white brick walls and shaped stone lintels exhibits minimal ecclesiastical detail. A limestone figure of St. Mark by Sheila Burlingame accents the facade. Burlingame, a native St. Louisan, was a pupil of internationally renowned sculptor Carl Milles. A collaboration of art and architecture is also found in noteworthy interior furnishings from St. Louis studios. They include an openwork steel lectern and pulpit by Clark Battle Fitzgerald, a handwoven hanging tapestry (originally installed on the altar steps) by Beatrice Root, a crucifix by Sheila Burlingame, and hanging

St. Mark's Episcopal, windows, c. 1940. Mercantile Library.

metal lamps by architects Nagel and Dunn.

The austere brick interior walls are relieved by a striking display of figural stained glass in pale shades of purple, blue, and green. Set in tall, slim windows, the glass was designed by Robert Harmon and executed by Emil Frei studios. The iconography of the eight nave windows derives from the Gospel of St. Mark. A stylized figure of Christ appears in the upper part of each window, unifying the series. The four north windows develop the theme of Mark's relationship with Christ; the south windows interpret the New Testament for the contemporary world and expound a social gospel. The first south window from the entrance illustrates the lesson of men

St. Mark's Episcopal, c. 1940. Mercantile Library.

mustached figure in another window reportedly is an allusion to Hitler.

The founding of St. Mark's parish was part of Bishop William Scarlett's strategy to combat declining membership in the city of St. Louis. The Episcopal diocese purchased St. Mark's site in 1932 for a mission church located in St. Louis Hills, a new subdivision (see #76) in southwest St. Louis. Upon completion of the present church in early 1939, St. Mark's parish was formed from the merger of the

cooperatively working together. This window also cryptically identifies the architects' names: Nagel is illustrated by a pun on the German word for nail while a workman holds a hammer with the name Dunn on it. Another south window depicts the self-destructive lust for power and money: branches grow bullets, money bags, skulls, and crossbones. In ominous symbolism foreshadowing World War II, a

St. Mark's Episcopal, c. 1940. St. Louis Public Library.

mission with two older parishes, Mt. Calvary and Holy Innocents.

Architect Charles Nagel (1899 - 1992) was born in St. Louis. He received three degrees from Yale University where he met Frederick Dunn (1905-1984), a native of St. Paul, Minnesota. The two architects formed a St. Louis partnership in 1936 which lasted until 1942, when Dunn entered the Navy. Nagel directed the Brooklyn Museum from 1946 to 1955, then returned to St. Louis as director of the Saint Louis Art Museum. He held that post from 1955 to 1964, before

St. Mark's Episcopal, statue, c. 1940. St. Louis Public Library.

becoming the first director of the National Portrait Gallery in Washington, D.C. Dunn remained in the architectural profession. Elegant reinterpretations of Georgian Revival became trademarks of his house and church designs. In 1962, Dunn was elected a Fellow of the American Institute of Architects for his body of St. Louis work. Singled out for citation were the National Council of State Garden Clubs headquarters at 4401 Magnolia in the Missouri Botanical Garden, Steinberg Skating Rink in Forest Park, and the Aloe warehouse at Lindbergh and Page Boulevards. In 1963, Dunn moved to New York and joined the architectural firm of Rogers, Butler & Bergun.

76. St. Gabriel the Archangel Roman Catholic Church

6303 Nottingham Avenue (at Tamm Avenue)
1950: Adolph F. Stauder & Arthur E. Stauder, St. Louis

In the midst of the Great Depression in 1934, about fifty Catholic families celebrated their first mass as St. Gabriel's parish in the crowded real estate office of Cyrus C. Willmore, the imaginative developer of St. Louis Hills. Willmore's extensive holdings once comprised the farm of David R. Francis - St. Louis Mayor, Missouri Governor, and U.S. Secretary of the

St. Gabriel the Archangel, c. 1951. Archdiocesan Archives.

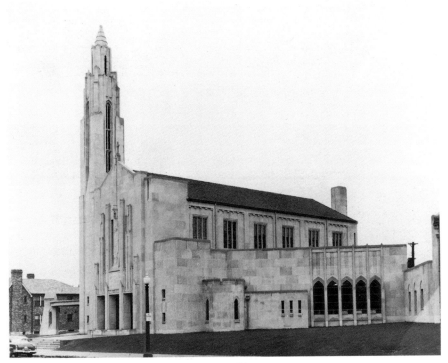

St. Gabriel the Archangel, c. 1951. Archdiocesan Archives.

Interior. Francis' donation of land for Francis Park, a 1930s WPA project, formed the centerpiece for Willmore's "country living in the city" promotions. In late 1934, the parish dedicated a one-story brick building designed by the Stauders; a second story was added after World War II. Meanwhile, the popular new neighborhood had mushroomed; model homes were featured as the "House of the Month" in *McCall's Magazine*. St. Gabriel's parish numbered 800 families by 1944.

Ground breaking for the new $600,000 church and rectory took place on March 5, 1950. Dedication by Archbishop Ritter was held in October 1951. According to the pastor, the design expressed a "modern traditional style, 'freshening up' traditional features rather than breaking with them completely." An exposed steel-trussed nave without columns offered a plan insuring that each of the 1,000 seats was not more than 80 feet from the altar. Restricted by a shallow lot, the centralized plan expanded laterally with fan-shaped wings.

The church, with a 12-story tower, features a relief-sculpture of St. Gabriel on the Bedford limestone facade. Modernistic clerestory windows display stylized angels in amber-white glass. On the east wall, five windows depict coats of arms of St. Louis Archdiocesan bishops from Rosati to Ritter. Arms of later bishops Carberry and May have been painted on the wall below. Italian pink marble on the interior walls was cut and polished in St. Louis.

A convent (completed in 1955) and the parish hall and gymnasium (from 1962) document continued growth. Today, St. Gabriel the Arch-angel is one of four churches facing Francis Park. The most recent arrival, St. Thomas Romanian Orthodox, is located on the site of Willmore's real estate office.

77. Resurrection Roman Catholic Church CL
3900 Meramec Street (at Hydraulic Avenue)
1952: Joseph D. Murphy (Murphy & Mackey), St. Louis

An innovative parabolic arch shape and avant garde litur-gical art made this building a benchmark of modern design in 1950s St. Louis. Guided by pastor George Dreher, design requirements called for an open, welcoming building that could comfortably seat 750 people "with an almost equal sense of nearness to the altar . . . the heart and focal point of the church." When completed in 1954 from de-signs by Joseph D. Murphy (1907-95) (then Dean of Washington University School of Architecture), a glass facade closing the ends of the parabola arch created an open-armed welcome. Tower placement at the apex of the

Resurrection Church. **Photo: Robert C. Pettus, 1989.** *Landmarks Association.*

parabola effectively marked the location of the altar that received additional emphasis inside through natural illumination from an oculus skylight. The request for a "prominently expressed" baptistery was met by a detached circular structure of lattice-like limestone and blue glass windows. Local artists, coordinated by the architect, provided interior decorations: clerestory art windows by Robert Frei, an altar mural by Robert Harmon, and sculpture by Hillis Arnold. Stations of the cross painted directly on an exposed brick wall were executed by William Schickel of Loveland, Ohio.

A Depression-era parish organized in 1930, Resurrection was carved out of the western end of St. Anthony of Padua's parish territory. The congregation first built a multi-purpose brick structure designed by Henry P. Hess. Still standing on Meramec Street, this $100,000 building housed classrooms, teachers' quarters, the rectory, a 600-seat chapel, plus bowling alleys and an auditorium in the basement. Post-World War II prosperity brought conditions favorable for the construction of the new church.

Architect Murphy received his undergraduate education at Rockhurst College in Kansas City. Exceptional graduate work at the Massachusetts Institute of Technology was marked first by the Fontainebleau scholarship which he won at age 22 for a year's study in France, followed by the Paris prize for an additional three and one-half years abroad. Back in his native Kansas City in 1932, Murphy worked on designs for the civic auditorium and the Jackson County courthouse with presiding judge Harry Truman breathing down his neck. Murphy first met Kenneth E. Wischmeyer as a new faculty member at Washington University in St. Louis. To the chagrin of many, the youthful pair won a citywide competition in 1937 to design the Muny Opera in Forest Park. Murphy entered into partnership with Eugene J. Mackey in 1952. The firm received the R. S. Reynolds Memorial Award in 1961 for their work on the Climatron at the Missouri Botanical Garden.

Church Survey Master List

ORIGINAL NAME	ORIGINAL DENOMINATION	ADDRESS	DATE
Quinn Chapel A.M.E.	A.M.E.	227 Bowen	c. 1868
St. Peter's A.M.E. Church	A.M.E.	2631 Elliott Avenue	1935
St. James A.M.E. Church	A.M.E.	4301 St. Ferdinand Avenue	1950-51
St. Mark's A.M.E. Church	A.M.E.	3514 Evans Avenue	1954
Apostolic Christian Church	Apostolic	815 Angelica Street	1914
Maplewood Apostolic Church	Apostolic	2199 Forest Avenue	1939
Berea Temple Assembly of God Church	Assembly of God	3224 Russell Boulevard	1954
Garrison Avenue Baptist Church	Baptist	620 Spring Avenue	1884
First German Baptist Church	Baptist	2629 Rauschenbach Avenue	1889
Lafayette Park Baptist Church	Baptist	1916 Lafayette Avenue	1889/1926
Delmar Baptist Church	Baptist	4300 Delmar Avenue	1891
Emmanuel Baptist Church	Baptist	5850 Cates Avenue	1892
Jefferson Avenue German Baptist Church	Baptist	2141 Jefferson Avenue	1892
Pilgrim Baptist Church	Baptist	4215 Kossuth Avenue	1895
Compton Hill Baptist Church	Baptist	3141 LaSalle Street	1900/1944
Taylor Avenue Baptist Church	Baptist	1260 North Euclid Avenue	c. 1902
Second Baptist Church	Baptist	500 North Kingshighway Boulevard	1907
Compton Heights Baptist Church	Baptist	3641 Russell Boulevard	1908
Corinthian Baptist Church	Baptist	447 Antelope Street	1909
Calvary Baptist Church	Baptist	4956 Emerson Avenue	1916
Grace Baptist Church	Baptist	2154 Bremen Avenue	1916
Delmar Baptist Church	Baptist	6195 Washington Boulevard	1918/1926
Antioch Baptist Church	Baptist	4213 West North Market Street	1920
Mt. Zion Baptist Church	Baptist	2765 LaSalle Street	1922/1948
Fourth Baptist Church	Baptist	2901 North Thirteenth Street	1923
Jewell Baptist Church	Baptist	3223 Osceola Street	1923
North Galilee Baptist Church	Baptist	2514 Leffingwell Avenue	1923/1971
Bethel Baptist Church	Baptist	5579 Labadie Avenue	1925
Euclid Baptist Church	Baptist	1341 North Kingshighway Boulevard	1925
West Park Baptist Church	Baptist	5988 Wells Avenue	1925

ORIGINAL NAME	ORIGINAL DENOMINATION	ADDRESS	DATE
New Tower Grove Baptist Church	Baptist	2911 Howard Street	1926/1953
Carondelet Baptist Church	Baptist	7309 Virginia Avenue	1928/1959
Water Tower Baptist Church	Baptist	2115 East Grand Boulevard	1936/1886
Southside Baptist Church	Baptist	3514 Oregon Avenue	1938
Corinthian Baptist Church	Baptist	6326 Colorado Avenue	1948
True-Light Baptist Church	Baptist	2838 James "Cool Papa" Bell Avenue	1948
West Florissant Baptist Church	Baptist	6080 West Florissant Avenue	1950
Third Baptist Church	Baptist	620 North Grand Boulevard	1951
Lindenwood Baptist Church	Baptist	6932 Lansdowne Avenue	1954
Lane Tabernacle C.M.E.	C.M.E.	3966 C. D. Banks Street	1903
Kennerly Temple C.O.G.I.C.	C.O.G.I.C.	4259 Kennerly Avenue	1929
Fifth Christian Church	Christian	1501 Penrose Street	1886
Compton Heights Christian Church	Christian	2800 St. Vincent Avenue	1894
Union Avenue Christian Church	Christian	733 Union Avenue	1904/1907
Hamilton Avenue Christian Church	Christian	1260 Hamilton Boulevard	1905
Strodtman Heights Christian Church	Christian	5547 Lilian Avenue	1905
Clifton Heights Christian Church	Christian	6420 Marmaduke Avenue	1909
Kingshighway Christian Church	Christian	3000 North Kingshighway Boulevard	1917
Spiritual Christian Union Church	Christian	4150 West Belle Place	1922
Dover Place Christian Church	Christian	701 Dover Place	1933
Oak Hill Chapel	Christian	4068 Parker Avenue	1948/1954
Compton Heights Christian Church	Christian	2149 South Grand Boulevard	1950
First Church of Christ, Scientist	Christian Science	475 North Kingshighway Boulevard	1903
Fourth Church of Christ, Scientist	Christian Science	5569 Page Boulevard	1909
Second Church of Christ, Scientist	Christian Science	4234 Washington Boulevard	1910/1953
Third Church of Christ, Scientist	Christian Science	3524 Russell Boulevard	1911
Sixth Church of Christ, Scientist	Christian Science	3736 Natural Bridge Avenue	1923
Eighth Church of Christ, Scientist	Christian Science	6221 Alexander Drive	1928
Fifth Church of Christ, Scientist	Christian Science	3458 Potomac Street	1928
Seventh Church of Christ, Scientist	Christian Science	1123 Holly Hills Ave./6336 Tennessee Ave.	1930
Second Church of Christ, Scientist	Christian Science	5807 Murdoch Avenue	1940
Cheltenham Church of Christ	Church of Christ	6234 Victoria Avenue	1911
Temple Church of Christ	Church of Christ	4146 Washington Boulevard	1948
Central Church of Christ	Church of Christ	305 South Skinker Boulevard	1951

ORIGINAL NAME	ORIGINAL DENOMINATION	ADDRESS	DATE
Morganford Church of Christ	Church of Christ	3551 Morganford Road	1954
Church of Christ	Church of Christ	4229 West Page Boulevard	1955
Church of God	Church of God	913 Garrison Avenue	1891/1908
First Congregational Church	Congregational	3610 Grandel Square	1884
Olive Branch Congregational Church	Congregational	2201 Sidney Street	1884
Third Congregational Church	Congregational	1220 North Grand Boulevard	1888
Compton Hill Congregational Church	Congregational	1640 South Compton Avenue	1893
Swedish Evangelical Congregational	Congregational	1201 Mackay Avenue	1894
Hyde Park Congregational Church	Congregational	1501 Bremen Avenue	1894/1903
Aubert Place Congregational Church	Congregational	4950 Fountain Avenue	1895
Pilgrim Congregational Church	Congregational	826 Union Avenue	1906
Hope Congregational Church	Congregational	1644 Semple Avenue	1913
Immanuel Congregational Church	Congregational	3460 Jamieson Avenue	1925
Central Christian Church	Disciples of Christ	3619 Finney Avenue	1887
Christ Church Episcopal	Episcopal	320 North Thirteenth Street	1859/1910
Holy Communion Episcopal Church	Episcopal	609 Leffingwell Avenue	1870/1876
St. John's Episcopal Church	Episcopal	1124 Dolman Street	1872
St. James Episcopal Church	Episcopal	1726 Annie Malone Drive	1888
St. Augustine Episcopal Church	Episcopal	7039 Bruno Avenue	1890
St. George's Episcopal Church	Episcopal	515 Pendleton Avenue	1891
St. Andrew's Episcopal Church	Episcopal	1428 North Garrison Avenue	1891/1928
Episcopal Church of the Redeemer	Episcopal	3010 Olive Street	1892
St. Mark's Episcopal Church	Episcopal	4005 Washington Boulevard	c. 1898
Good Shepherd Episcopal Mission Church	Episcopal	2838 Salena Street	1899
St. James Memorial Church	Episcopal	600 North Euclid Avenue	1900/'54/'62
St. John's Episcopal Church	Episcopal	3664 Arsenal Street	1907
St. Philip the Apostle Episcopal Church	Episcopal	1244 Union Boulevard	1911
St. Paul's Episcopal Church	Episcopal	6516 Michigan Avenue	1912
Grace Hill Episcopal Church	Episcopal	2529 North Eleventh Street	1923
St. Mark's Episcopal Church	Episcopal	4712 Clifton Avenue	1939
Carondelet German Evangelical Church	Evangelical	7423 Michigan Avenue	1871/1902
St. James German Evangelical Church	Evangelical	1507 East College Avenue	1887
St. Matthew's German Evangelical Church	Evangelical	2613 Potomac Street	1888
Christ Evangelical Church	Evangelical	7121 Manchester Avenue	1891

ORIGINAL NAME	ORIGINAL DENOMINATION	ADDRESS	DATE
Trinity Church	Evangelical	3124 Mt. Pleasant Street	1894/1904
Jesus Evangelical Church	Evangelical	2420 South Twelfth Street	1895
St. Paul's Evangelical Congregation	Evangelical	1808 South Ninth Street	1896
Emmaus Evangelical Church	Evangelical	4347 Chouteau Avenue	1897
Salem Evangelical Church	Evangelical	4730 Margaretta Avenue	1898
Bethel English Evangelical Church	Evangelical	2941 Greer Avenue	1904/1907
Evangelische Synode	Evangelical	3550 Morganford Road	1905
Deutsche Evangelische Friedens Kirche	Evangelical	1908 Newhouse Avenue	1907
Evangelische St. Petri Kirche	Evangelical	4015 St. Louis Avenue	1909
St. Luke's Evangelical Church	Evangelical	2336 Tennessee Avenue	1912
Bethany Evangelical Church	Evangelical	4449 Red Bud Avenue	1913-14
St. Marcus German Evangelical Church	Evangelical	2102 Russell Boulevard	1914
Independent Evangelical Church	Evangelical	4001 Fair Avenue	1916
Eden Emanuel Church	Evangelical	1247 Temple Place	1921
Evangelical Church of the Redeemer	Evangelical	6446 South Kingshighway Boulevard	1921/1930
Pilgrim Evangelical Church	Evangelical	3325 Arsenal Street	1922
St. John's Evangelical Church	Evangelical	4138 North Grand Boulevard	1922
Holy Ghost Evangelical Church	Evangelical	4916 Mardell Avenue	1927/1950
Italian Evangelical Church	Evangelical	5343 Botanical Avenue	1928
Trinity Evangelical Church	Evangelical	4700 South Grand Boulevard	1930
St. Paul's Evangelical Church	Evangelical	3660 Potomac Street	1931
St. Stephen Evangelical Church	Evangelical	8500 Halls Ferry Road	1937
Grace Evangelical & Reformed Church	Evangelical	5712 Leona Street	1940/1963
Mt. Tabor Evangelical Reformed Church	Evangelical	6520 Arsenal Street	1949
Salvator Evangelical Reformed Church	Evangelical	5618 Thekla Avenue	1950
Hope Evangelical and Reformed Church	Evangelical	6273 Eichelberger Street	1955
St. Paul's Evangelical Friedens Church	Friedens Church	2010 South Thirteenth Street	1886
B'nai El Temple	Jewish	3666 Flad Avenue	1905
Temple Israel	Jewish	5001 Washington Boulevard	1907
Shaare Zedek	Jewish	4570 Page Boulevard	1914
B'nai Amoona Congregation	Jewish	1212 Academy Avenue	1918
United Hebrew Congregation Temple	Jewish	225 South Skinker Boulevard	1924
Blaine Avenue Tabernacle	Jewish	4200 Blaine Avenue	1927
Beth Abraham Congregational Synagogue	Jewish	1444 Goodfellow Boulevard	1929

ORIGINAL NAME	ORIGINAL DENOMINATION	ADDRESS	DATE
Congregation Zephron David	Jewish	1488 Belt Avenue	1930
Church of Jesus Christ of Latter Day Saints	Latter Day Saints	4720 Jamieson Avenue	1949
Zion German Evangelical Lutheran Church	Lutheran	1428 Warren Street	1860
Holy Cross Lutheran Church	Lutheran	2650 Miami Street	1867/1889
St. Trinity Lutheran Church	Lutheran	7404 Vermont Avenue	1872
St. Mark's English Lutheran Church	Lutheran	3100 Bell Avenue	1881
Christ Lutheran Church	Lutheran	3504 Caroline Street	1886-1887
Bethlehem Lutheran Church	Lutheran	2153 Salisbury Street	1894
Zion German Evangelical Lutheran Church	Lutheran	2500 North Twenty-first Street	1895
Trinity German Evangelical Lutheran	Lutheran	1805 South Eighth Street	1896
English Lutheran Church of Our Redeemer	Lutheran	3127 California Avenue	1897
Emmaus Evangelical Lutheran Church	Lutheran	2235 Jefferson Avenue	1901
St. Paul's English Evangelical Lutheran	Lutheran	1034 South Kingshighway Boulevard	1906
St. Peter's German Evangelical Lutheran	Lutheran	1211 South Newstead Avenue	1907
Evang. Lutheran Church of Our Redeemer	Lutheran	2827 Utah Street	1908
St. Luke's Lutheran Church	Lutheran	3415 Taft Avenue	1909
Grace Evangelical Lutheran U.A.C.	Lutheran	3117 St. Louis Avenue	1912
Pilgrim Evangelical Lutheran Church	Lutheran	4112 West Florissant Avenue	1912
St. Matthew's Lutheran Congregation	Lutheran	5503 Gilmore Avenue	1912
Marcus (St. Mark's) Evang. Lutheran	Lutheran	4042 North Twenty-second Street	1912/1950
Mt. Calvary Evangelical Lutheran	Lutheran	1444 Union Boulevard	1913
Ebenezer Lutheran Church	Lutheran	1005 Theobald Street	1922
St. Paul's Evangelical Lutheran Church	Lutheran	2137 East John Street	1924-25
St. Peter's Lutheran Church	Lutheran	1126 South Kingshighway Boulevard	1925
Immanuel Lutheran Church	Lutheran	3530 Marcus Avenue	1927
Bethany Evangelical Lutheran Church	Lutheran	4100 Natural Bridge Avenue	1928
St. Matthew Lutheran Church U. A. C.	Lutheran	5402 Wren Avenue	1928
Messiah Lutheran Church	Lutheran	2846 South Grand Boulevard	1929
Faith Evangelical Lutheran Church	Lutheran	2821 North Kingshighway Boulevard	1930
Hope Lutheran Church	Lutheran	5222 Neosho Street	1930
Lutheran Church of Our Savior	Lutheran	2854 Abner Place	1931
Mt. Olive Lutheran Church	Lutheran	4246 Shaw Boulevard	1931
Ascension Lutheran Church	Lutheran	6501 Eichelberger Street	1940/1981
St. Philip's Lutheran Church	Lutheran	4000 West Belle Place	1944

ORIGINAL NAME	ORIGINAL DENOMINATION	ADDRESS	DATE
Swedish Evangelical Lutheran Church	Lutheran	3600 Hampton Avenue	1947
Epiphany Lutheran Church	Lutheran	4045 Holly Hills Boulevard	1947/1954
St. John Lutheran Church	Lutheran	3738 Morganford Road	1948
Advent Evangelical Lutheran Church	Lutheran	3752 Giles Avenue	1952
St. John's Methodist Church, South	Methodist	2901 Locust Boulevard	1867
Centenary M. E. Church, South	Methodist	55 Plaza Square	1868
Union Methodist Church	Methodist	613 North Garrison Avenue	1880
Cook Avenue M.E. Church, South	Methodist	3680 Cook Avenue	1884
Lafayette Park M.E. Church, South	Methodist	2300 Lafayette Avenue	1887/1900
Carondelet Methodist Church	Methodist	426 Blow Street	1890
Eden Methodist Episcopal Church	Methodist	5987 Wabada Avenue	1891
Marvin Chapel	Methodist	2526 South Twelfth Street	1891
St. Paul's German Methodist Church	Methodist	2921 McNair Avenue	1891
Memorial Methodist Episcopal Church	Methodist	2157 Jefferson Avenue	1892/1896
Wagoner Place Methodist Church	Methodist	1527 Dick Gregory Place	c. 1894
Lindell Avenue Methodist Church	Methodist	340 North Skinker Boulevard	1896/1913
German Zion Methodist Episcopal Church	Methodist	7425 Virginia Avenue	1897
St. John's Methodist Episcopal Church	Methodist	5000 Washington Place	1901
Cabanne Methodist Episcopal Church	Methodist	5760 Bartmer Avenue	1902
St. Paul's Methodist Episcopal Church	Methodist	1927 St. Louis Avenue	1902
Carondelet M.E. Church, South	Methodist	6701 Virginia Avenue	1903
Elmbank M.E. Church (German)	Methodist	4437 Elmbank Avenue	1903
Tower Grove Methodist Episcopal Church	Methodist	1040 South Taylor Avenue	1903
Fry Memorial Methodist Episcopal Church	Methodist	2501 Clifton Avenue	1905
Salem Methodist Church	Methodist	4301 Page Boulevard	1905
Wesley Chapel, M.E. Church of Baden	Methodist	8375 North Broadway	1905
Zoar Methodist Episcopal Church	Methodist	4300 Gano Avenue	1906/1925
Chouteau Place Methodist Church	Methodist	4001 Maffitt Avenue	1909
Walnut Park Methodist Episcopal Church	Methodist	6100 Emma Avenue	1913/1925
Christy Memorial U. M. Church	Methodist	4601 Morganford Road	1914
Lighthouse Memorial Mission	Methodist	1218 Tower Grove Avenue	1914
St. James Chapel M.E. Church	Methodist	4214 West Papin Street	c. 1915
Bowman Methodist Episcopal Church	Methodist	4276 Athlone Avenue	1920
Arlington M. E. Church, South	Methodist	2801 Union Boulevard	1921

ORIGINAL NAME	ORIGINAL DENOMINATION	ADDRESS	DATE
Samaritan Methodist Episcopal Church	Methodist	4168 West Belle Place	1922
Free Methodist Church	Methodist	5075 Davison Avenue	1924
Salem Methodist Episcopal Church	Methodist	1908 North Kingshighway Boulevard	1924
Kingshighway United Methodist Church	Methodist	900 Bellerive Boulevard	1925
Flower Memorial Methodist Church	Methodist	1324 Tower Grove Avenue	1927
Immanuel M.E. Church, South	Methodist	2105 McCausland Avenue	1927
Scruggs Memorial U. M. Church	Methodist	3443 Grace Avenue	1929
Taylor Chapel Colored Methodist Church	Methodist	3305 Hickory Street	1947
Christ Methodist Church	Methodist	6501 Pernod Avenue	1949/1954
LaSalle United Methodist Church	Methodist	1024 Montrose Avenue	1952
Shaw Avenue United Methodist Church	Methodist	4265 Shaw Boulevard	1952
Pilgrim Rest Missionary Baptist Church	Missionary Baptist	2900 Gamble Street	1878
Emanuel Missionary Baptist Church	Missionary Baptist	2735 Thomas Street	1922/1941
Bethel Temple	Missionary Baptist	3529 North Jefferson	c. 1927
New Hope Missionary Baptist Church	Missionary Baptist	1428 Biddle Street	1944
Prince of Peace M.B. Church	Missionary Baptist	2741 Dayton Street	1948
Newstead Avenue M.B. Church	Missionary Baptist	4362 North Market	1950
Northernstar Missionary Baptist Church	Missionary Baptist	2614 James "Cool Papa" Bell Avenue	1953
Trinity Mt. Carmel M.B. Church	Missionary Baptist	1819 North Prairie Avenue	1953
Holy Trinity Serbian Eastern Orthodox	Orthodox, Eastern	1910 McNair Avenue	1928
St. Nicholas Greek Orthodox Church	Orthodox, Greek	4967 Forest Park Avenue	1930
St. Michael the Archangel Russian Orth.	Orthodox, Russian	1901 Ann Avenue	1928
True Vine Spiritual Church	Other	3911 West Belle Place	c. 1915
North Presbyterian Church	Presbyterian	2005 North Eleventh Street	1857
Carondelet Presbyterian Church	Presbyterian	6116 Michigan Avenue	1863/1895
First German Presbyterian Church	Presbyterian	1000 Rutger Street	1871
Washington & Compton Ave. Presbyterian	Presbyterian	3200 Washington Boulevard	1877
Lafayette Park Presbyterian Church	Presbyterian	1505 Missouri Avenue	1881-83
German Cumberland Presbyterian	Presbyterian	2347 Sullivan Avenue	1884
First Presbyterian Church	Presbyterian	4100 Washington Boulevard	1888
Clifton Heights Presbyterian Church	Presbyterian	6201 Columbia Avenue	c. 1891
Lane Tabernacle C.M.E. Church	Presbyterian	910 North Newstead Avenue	1893
Wagoner Place United Presbyterian	Presbyterian	1915 Dick Gregory Place	1893
Cote Brilliante Presbyterian Church	Presbyterian	4673 Labadie Avenue	1894

ORIGINAL NAME	ORIGINAL DENOMINATION	ADDRESS	DATE
Second Presbyterian Church	Presbyterian	4501 Westminster Place	1896/1899
Curby Memorial Presbyterian Church	Presbyterian	2621 Utah Street	1897
Grace Presbyterian Church	Presbyterian	5601 Ridge Avenue	1901/1909
Tyler Place United Presbyterian Church	Presbyterian	2109 South Spring Avenue	1901
Compton Hill Chapel	Presbyterian	3116 St. Vincent Avenue	1902/1910
Brank Memorial Presbyterian Church	Presbyterian	1212 Academy Avenue	1904
Second German Presbyterian	Presbyterian	1524 East Grand Boulevard	1906
Central Presbyterian Church	Presbyterian	5574 Delmar Avenue	1907
Kingshighway Cumberland Presbyterian	Presbyterian	5010 Cabanne Avenue	1908
Gibson Heights United Presbyterian	Presbyterian	1075 South Taylor Avenue	1910
West Presbyterian Church	Presbyterian	967 Maryville Avenue	1911/1916
Lee Avenue Presbyterian Church	Presbyterian	3950 Carter Avenue	1913
Oak Hill Presbyterian Church	Presbyterian	4111 Connecticut Street	1914
Third Presbyterian Church	Presbyterian	2426 Union Boulevard	1915
Grand Avenue Presbyterian Church	Presbyterian	5300 Delmar Boulevard	1916
North Presbyterian Church	Presbyterian	4015 St. Louis Avenue	1917
Winnebago Presbyterian Church	Presbyterian	3436 Winnebago Street	1921
St. Paul's Presbyterian Church	Presbyterian	5209 Lilian Avenue	1922
University Presbyterian Church	Presbyterian	6166 Delmar Boulevard	1924
Memorial Presbyterian Church	Presbyterian	201 South Skinker Boulevard	1925/1931
Southhampton Presbyterian Church	Presbyterian	4716 Macklind Avenue	1925/1941
McCausland Avenue Presbyterian Church	Presbyterian	1517 McCausland Avenue	1927
St. Louis Presbyterian Church	Presbyterian	2240 St. Louis Avenue	1929
Peters Memorial Presbyterian Church	Presbyterian	3100 Sidney Street	1931
Brandt Memorial Presbyterian Church	Presbyterian	4523 Rosa Avenue	1949
Reformed Church of the United States	Ref. Church of US	1246 Clarendon Avenue	1899
Basilica of St. Louis, King of France	Roman Catholic	209 Walnut Street	1831
St. Mary of Victories R.C. Church	Roman Catholic	744 South Third Street	1843/1859
St. Vincent de Paul R.C. Church	Roman Catholic	1417 South Ninth Street	1844
St. Bridget of Erin R.C. Church	Roman Catholic	1100 North Jefferson Avenue	1859
St. John the Apostle/Evangelist R.C.	Roman Catholic	15 Plaza Square	1859
St. Boniface Roman Catholic Church	Roman Catholic	7622 Michigan Avenue	1860
St. Joseph's Roman Catholic Church	Roman Catholic	1220 North Eleventh Street	1865/1880
St. Alphonsus Roman Catholic Church	Roman Catholic	1118 North Grand Boulevard	1867/1893

ORIGINAL NAME	ORIGINAL DENOMINATION	ADDRESS	DATE
SS. Peter & Paul R.C. Church	Roman Catholic	1919 South Seventh Boulevard	1873
St. Cronan's Roman Catholic Church	Roman Catholic	1203 South Boyle Avenue	1879
St. Thomas of Aquin R.C. Church	Roman Catholic	3949 Iowa Avenue	1882
St. Francis Xavier R.C. Church	Roman Catholic	3628 Lindell Boulevard	1884
St. Agatha Roman Catholic Church	Roman Catholic	3239 South Ninth Street	1884/1899
St. Liborius Roman Catholic Church	Roman Catholic	1835 North Eighteenth Street	1889/1907
St. Agnes Roman Catholic Church	Roman Catholic	1935 Sidney Street	1890
St. Stanislaus Kostka R.C. Church	Roman Catholic	1415 North Twentieth Street	1891
Our Lady of Good Counsel Conv. Chapel	Roman Catholic	1849 Cass Avenue	1896
St. Augustine's Roman Catholic Church	Roman Catholic	3114 Lismore Street	1896/1928
Most Holy Trinity R.C. Church	Roman Catholic	3519 North Fourteenth Street	1897
Sisters of St. Joseph/Carondelet Chapel	Roman Catholic	6400 Minnesota Avenue	1897
St. John Nepomuk Catholic Church	Roman Catholic	1631 South Eleventh Street	1897
Former St. Aloysius Gonzaga R.C. Church	Roman Catholic	2645 Pearl Avenue	1899
St. Teresa of Avila R.C. Church	Roman Catholic	2413 North Grand Boulevard	1899
St. Mark's Roman Catholic Church	Roman Catholic	1313 Academy Avenue	1901
Holy Cross Roman Catholic Church	Roman Catholic	8115 Church Road	1903
Immaculate Conception R.C. Church	Roman Catholic	3120 Lafayette Avenue	1904
St. Hedwig's R.C. Church & School	Roman Catholic	3214 Pulaski Street	1904
Nativity of Our Lord R.C. Church	Roman Catholic	5501 Oriole Avenue	1905
St. Barbara's Roman Catholic Church	Roman Catholic	5909 Minerva Avenue	1905
St. Anthony of Padua R.C. Church	Roman Catholic	3134 Meramec Street	1906
St. Margaret of Scotland R.C. Church	Roman Catholic	3854 Flad Avenue	1906
St. Matthew's Roman Catholic Church	Roman Catholic	2715 North Sarah Street	1906
Cathedral of St. Louis (New Cathedral)	Roman Catholic	4431 Lindell Boulevard	1907
St. Francis de Sales R.C. Church	Roman Catholic	2653 Ohio Street	1907
Visitation Church	Roman Catholic	4515 Evans Avenue	1908
St. Henry's Roman Catholic Church	Roman Catholic	1230 California	1909
St. Rose's Roman Catholic Church	Roman Catholic	1001 Goodfellow Boulevard	1909
St. Ann Roman Catholic Church	Roman Catholic	1220 Whittier Street	1910
Society of Helpers of the Holy Souls	Roman Catholic	4012 Washington Boulevard	1910/1920s
St. Edward the King R.C. Church	Roman Catholic	2701 Clara Avenue	1912
Blessed Sacrament R.C. Church	Roman Catholic	5017 Maffitt Avenue	1914
Holy Name Roman Catholic Church	Roman Catholic	2041 East Grand Boulevard	1916

ORIGINAL NAME	ORIGINAL DENOMINATION	ADDRESS	DATE
Pope St. Pius V R.C. Church	Roman Catholic	3310 South Grand Boulevard	1916
St. Roch's Roman Catholic Church	Roman Catholic	6052 Waterman Boulevard	1921
Holy Rosary Roman Catholic Church	Roman Catholic	3905 Clarence Avenue	1922
St. John the Baptist R.C. Church	Roman Catholic	4200 Delor Street	1924
Church of the Holy Family	Roman Catholic	4123 Humphrey Street	1925
St. Aloysius Gonzaga R.C. Church	Roman Catholic	2645 Pearl Avenue	1925
St. Ambrose Roman Catholic Church	Roman Catholic	5130 Wilson Avenue	1925
St. Wenceslaus Roman Catholic Church	Roman Catholic	3006 Oregon Avenue	1925
St. Cecilia Roman Catholic Church	Roman Catholic	5401 Alaska Avenue	1926
St. Engelbert Roman Catholic Church	Roman Catholic	4330 Shreve Avenue	1926
Mt. Grace Chapel of Perpetual Adoration	Roman Catholic	1438 East Warne Avenue	1927
Our Lady of Sorrows R.C. Church	Roman Catholic	5831 South Kingshighway Boulevard	1927
St. James the Greater R.C. Church	Roman Catholic	1345 Tamm Avenue	1927
St. Joseph Croatian R.C. Church	Roman Catholic	2100 South Twelfth Street	1927-1928
Epiphany of Our Lord R.C. Church	Roman Catholic	6598 Smiley Avenue	1929
St. Philip Neri Roman Catholic Church	Roman Catholic	5076 Durant Avenue	1931
Firmin Desloges Hospital Chapel	Roman Catholic	1325 South Grand Boulevard	1933
Monsignor McGlenn Memorial Chapel	Roman Catholic	4745 South Grand Boulevard	1936
Our Lady of Mt. Carmel R.C. Church	Roman Catholic	8747 Annetta Street	1938
SS. Mary and Joseph R.C. Church	Roman Catholic	6304 Minnesota Avenue	1940
St. Mary Magdalen R.C. Church	Roman Catholic	4924 Bancroft Avenue	1940
St. Gabriel the Archangel R.C. Church	Roman Catholic	6303 Nottingham Avenue	1950
Immaculate Heart of Mary R.C. Church	Roman Catholic	4092 Blow Street	1952
Resurrection Roman Catholic Church	Roman Catholic	3900 Meramec Street	1952
St. Adalbert Roman Catholic Church	Roman Catholic	5720 Woodland Avenue	1955
South Seventh Day Adventist Church	7th Day Adventist	3458 Minnesota Avenue	1915
Berean Seventh Day Adventist Church	7th Day Adventist	1208 North Sarah Street	1931
Southside Seventh Day Adventist Church	7th Day Adventist	3963 Chipppewa Street	1937
Ephesus Seventh Day Adventist Church	7th Day Adventist	1900 Whittier Street	1946
Society of Practical Christianity	Soc. of Prac. Chris.	3617 Wyoming Street	1916
Burkett Spiritualist Church	Spiritualist	2653 Natural Bridge Avenue	1941
Second German Swedenborgian Church	Swedenborgian	2126 St. Louis Avenue	1883
Church of the Unity	Unitarian	1322 Mackay Avenue	1870
Church of the Messiah Unitarian	Unitarian	800 North Union Boulevard	1907

ORIGINAL NAME	ORIGINAL DENOMINATION	ADDRESS	DATE
Church of the Unity	Unitarian	5007 Waterman Boulevard	1916
South Side Unity Society	Unity Society	3616 Bates Street	1941
Gospel Hall	Unknown	7138 Southwest Avenue	1922

Detail: Shrine of St. Joseph, c. 1980. Landmarks collection.

Selected Bibliography

This bibliography contains titles found in the collections of the St. Louis Public Library. While not all titles are listed in the catalog, most may be found in the Rare Books & Special Collections Department. Other materials on religion and churches in the St. Louis area are also available in St. Louis Public Library collections.

Works on St. Louis history, background material, and general religious surveys are listed first. These are followed by titles grouped according to religious denomination, then those grouped by church or synagogue.

GENERAL BIBLIOGRAPHY

Barry, David W. *The Protestant Churches of St. Louis and St. Louis County, Missouri: A Study of Social Change and Church Trends.* [St. Louis]: The Metropolitan Church Federation of St. Louis, Committee for Cooperative Field Research, 1947.

Bryan, John Albury. *Missouri's Contribution to American Architecture; A History of the Architectural Achievements in This State From the Time of the Earliest Settlements Down to the Present Year.* [St. Louis: Saint Louis Architectural Club], 1928.

Churches of St. Louis. [St. Louis: Municipal Reference Library, n.d.].
A collection of clippings, mostly from the *St. Louis Star-Times,* the *St. Louis Post-Dispatch,* and the *St. Louis Globe-Democrat,* from the 1930s though the 1960s, compiled by the Municipal Reference Library, St. Louis Public Library.

Coyle, Elinor M. *Saint Louis, Portrait of a River City.* 3rd ed. St. Louis: Folkestone Press, 1977.

---. *Saint Louis Treasures: Photographs and Text.* St. Louis: Folkestone Press, 1986.

Douglass, Harlan Paul. *The St. Louis Church Survey; A Religious Investigation With a Social Background.* New York: George H. Doran Company, 1924.

Dry, Camille N. *Pictorial St. Louis; A Topographical Survey Drawn in Perspective, 1875.* Edited by R. J. Compton. St. Louis, 1876.

Hannon, Robert E., comp. and ed. *St. Louis: Its Neighborhoods and Neighbors, Landmarks and Milestones.* St. Louis: Regional Commerce and Growth Association, 1986.

Harris, Eileen NiNi. *A Grand Heritage: A History of the St. Louis Southside Neighborhoods and Citizens.* [St. Louis]: DeSales Community Housing Corp., 1984.

---. *A History of Carondelet.* St. Louis: Patrice Press, 1991.

Hyde, William, and Howard L. Conard, eds. *Encyclopedia of the History of St. Louis, A Compendium of History and Biography for Ready Reference.* 4 vols. New York: The Southern History Company, 1899.

Linderer, Nanette M. *St. Louis Churches.* N.p.: n.p., [1973?].

McCue, George. *The Building Art in St. Louis; Two Centuries: A Guide to Architecture of the City and its Metropolitan Region.* 3rd ed. St. Louis: Knight, 1981.

Oestreich, Kenneth D., and Norbury L. Wayman. *St. Louis Landmarks: A Guide to the City's Landmarks & Historic Districts.* St. Louis: Community Development Agency, 1977.

Peters, Frank, and George McCue. *A Guide to the Architecture of St. Louis.* St. Louis: St. Louis Chapter, American Institute of Architects; Columbia: University of Missouri Press, 1989.

Primm, James Neal. *Lion of the Valley: Saint Louis, Missouri.* 2nd ed. Boulder, Colo.: Pruett Pub. Co., 1990.

Scharf, J. Thomas. *History of Saint Louis City and County, From the Earliest Periods to the Present Day: Including Biographical Sketches of Representative Men.* 2 vols. Philadelphia: L.H. Everts & Co., 1883.

Smith, JoAnn Adams. *Selected Neighbors and Neighborhoods of North St. Louis and Selected Related Events.* St. Louis: Friends of the Vaughn Cultural Center, 1988.

Toft, Carolyn Hewes. *St. Louis: Landmarks & Historic Districts.* St. Louis: Landmarks Association of St. Louis, 1988.

Van Ravensway, Charles. *Saint Louis: An Informal History of the City and Its People, 1764-1865.* Ed. Candace O'Connor. St. Louis: Missouri Historical Society, 1991.

BAPTIST

Duncan, R. S. *A History of the Baptists in Missouri: Embracing an Account of the Organization and Growth of Baptist Churches and Associations; Biographical Sketches of Ministers of the Gospel and Other Prominent Members of the Denomination; the Founding Baptist Institutions, Periodicals, etc.* Lafayette, Tenn: Church History Research & Archives, [1981, 1882].

Truex, Harvey Eldon. *Baptists in Missouri; Being a Brief Account of the Early Struggles, the Organization, etc., of the Denomination in the State.* [Columbia, Mo.: Press of E. W. Stephens, 1904].

CENTRAL BAPTIST

Huntley, Elizabeth Maddox. *A History of Central Baptist Church, 1942-1982: Revealing the Local, National and International Impact of Her Ministries.* St. Louis, 1988.

Stevens, George E. *History of the Central Baptist Church, Showing Her Influence Upon Her Times.* St. Louis: King Pub., 1927.

DELMAR BAPTIST

Norman, Elva Kuykendall. *Biography of a Church: A History of the Early St. Louis Baptist Community, 1817-1877, and Delmar Church Which Emerged From It, 1877-1977.* St. Louis, 1978.

THIRD BAPTIST

Dedication Program, October Eighteenth Through Twenty-Fifth, Nineteen Hundred and Forty-Two. [St. Louis: Third Baptist Church, 1942?].

Third Baptist Church, Saint Louis, 1850-1920: Condensed History of Seventy Years . . . Report of Activities During the Year of 1920. Prepared by A.W. Payne, W.C. Teasdale and W.C. Ayer. St. Louis: Buschart Brothers Printing Co., [1921].

WEST PARK BAPTIST

Fiftieth Anniversary of the West Park Baptist Church, Hodiamont and Wells Avenues, Saint Louis, Missouri, 1893-1943. [St. Louis, 1943?].

CATHOLIC

Brien, Manson Milner. *One Hundred Years in the Diocese of Missouri.* [St. Louis: n.p., 1940].

Conway, James Joseph. *The Beginnings of Ecclesiastical Jurisdiction: In the Archdiocese of St. Louis, 1764-1776.* St. Louis: Missouri Historical Society, 1897.

Faherty, William Barnaby. *Dream by the River: Two Centuries of Saint Louis Catholicism, 1766-1980.* St. Louis: River City Publishers, 1981.

Historic Churches in St. Louis: Self-Guided Tour. St. Louis: Archdiocesan Council of the Laity, [ca. 1976].

James, Ivan C., Jr. *The History of Black Catholicism in St. Louis.* [St. Louis: St. Charles Lwanga Center, n.d.].

Rothensteiner, Johannes. *History of the Archdiocese of St. Louis: In Its Various Stages of Development From A.D. 1673 to A.D. 1928.* St. Louis: Blackwell Wielandy, 1928.

St. Louis Catholic Historical Review. 5 vols. St. Louis: Catholic Historical Society of St. Louis, 1918-23.

Schulte, Paul C. *The Catholic Heritage of Saint Louis: A History of the Old Cathedral Parish, St. Louis, Mo.* St. Louis: [Printed by the *Catholic Herald*], 1974.

Thornton, Francis A. *The Notable Catholic Institutions of Saint Louis and Vicinity:* [With a Sketch on the New Cathedral, by G.D. Barnett.] [St. Louis: n.p, 1911].

NEW CATHEDRAL

Faherty, William Barnaby. *The Great Saint Louis Cathedral.* St. Louis: Archdiocese of Saint Louis, 1988.

Reinforced-Concrete Co., St. Louis. *Structural Reinforced-Concrete in the New Cathedral for the Archepiscopal See of St. Louis.* [St. Louis: Brussel & Viterbo, Consulting Engineers for the Reinforced-Concrete Co., 1911].

The St. Louis Cathedral; A Photographic Sketch. Rev. ed. St. Louis, 1948. Library has earlier editions.

Walsh, John G., ed. *The Cathedral of Saint Louis.* St. Louis, [1964?.]

OLD CATHEDRAL

Arteaga, Robert F. *The Old Cathedral, St. Louis Basilica, St. Louis, Mo.* St. Louis: St. Louis IX Basilica Historical Society, 1968.

Behrmann, Elmer H. *The Story of the Old Cathedral Parish of St. Louis IX, King of France, St. Louis, Mo.* St. Louis: Church of St. Louis IX, King of France, 1949.
A supplement was published in 1964.

Bryan, John Albury. *An Architectural and Historical Sketch of the Old Cathedral.* [St. Louis]: U.S. Dept. of the Interior, National Park Service, Jefferson National Expansion Memorial, 1957.

Franzwa, Gregory M. *The Old Cathedral.* 2nd ed. Gerald, Mo.: Patrice Press, 1980.

HOLY CROSS

A Souvenir of the Diamond Jubilee of Holy Cross Parish, 1864-1939, Saint Louis, Missouri. [St. Louis, 1939].

ST. ALPHONSUS

St. Alphonsus Church. *Leaves From the History of St. Alphonsus Church, St. Louis, Mo., 1875: Compiled in Commemoration of the Completion of the Church.* St. Louis: Carreras, 1895.

ST. AMBROSE

St. Ambrose Church. *Fortieth Anniversary; Historical Review, Brief Historical Sketches and Data of Saint Ambrose Parish, Marconi and Wilson Avenues, St. Louis, Mo., U.S.A.: Past and Present Achievements by Italians in America, 1903-1943.* [St. Louis: Boggiano Bros. Printing Co., 1943].

---. *Nuova Chiesa Italiana di Sant' Ambroglio: Dedicata il 27 Giugno, 1926.* St. Louis: Boggiano Bros., [1926?].

---. *Souvenir Program of the Jubilee Celebrations in Honor of Father Lupo: For the Benefit of St. Ambrose New School, Sunday, Aug. 8-15, 1937.* [St. Louis, 1937].

ST. ANTHONY

Poppy, Maximus, O.F.M. *A Guide to the Ecclesiastical Art in St. Anthony's Church, St. Louis, Mo.* St. Louis, n.d.

St. Anthony of Padua Church. *Souvenir of the Diamond Jubilee of St. Anthony Parish, 1863-1938, Saint Louis, Missouri.* [St. Louis, 1938].

ST. FRANCIS DE SALES

St. Francis de Sales Parish 125th Anniversary, 1867-1992. [St. Louis? 1992].

St. Francis de Sales Parish and Church. [Dave Cuevas, NiNi Harris, Alec Burrell]. [St. Louis? 1994].

ST. FRANCIS XAVIER

The Stained Glass: St. Francis Xavier Church, St. Louis. [St. Louis, n.d.].

ST. JAMES THE GREATER

St. James the Greater Church, 1861-1986. [St. Louis, 1986?]

O'Connor, P. J. *History of Cheltenham and St. James Parish: Commemorating the Diamond Jubilee of St. James Parish and the Twenty-Fifth Anniversary of the Coming to the Parish of Rev. P. J. O'Connor, Pastor.* [St. Louis, 1937].

ST. JOHN NEPOMUK

St. John Nepomuk Church. *Souvenir of Diamond Jubilee, St. John Nepomuk Parish, Sunday, Nov. 24, to Thursday, Nov. 28, 1929.* St. Louis, [1929].

ST. ROCH'S

Eberle, Jean Fahey. *Saint Roch's: The Story of a Parish.* [St. Louis: St. Roch's Catholic Church, 1967?]

SHRINE OF ST. JOSEPH

Jensen, Mrs. Dana O. *"Historic St. Joseph's."* Missouri Historical Society Bulletin 19 (1963): 273-276.

CHRISTIAN CHURCHES

UNION AVENUE CHRISTIAN CHURCH

For Where Your Treasure Is . . . There Will Your Heart Be Also. [St. Louis, 194-?].
Outlines plans for church expansion.

On the Threshold of Greatness. St. Louis: Union Avenue Christian Church, n.d.

EPISCOPAL

ALL SAINTS EPISCOPAL

All Saints Parish. *A Memorial From All Saints Parish, Garrison Ave. and Locust Street, St. Louis, Mo.: Protesting Against the Proposal of a Racial Episcopate.* [St. Louis], 1916.

CHRIST CHURCH CATHEDRAL

Christ Church Cathedral. *Centennial Christ Church Cathedral, Saint Louis, 1819-1919.* [St. Louis, 1919?].

---. *Report of the Centennial Celebration, 1819-1919.* [St. Louis], 1919.

Christ Church Cathedral. *Yearbook.* St. Louis, [1889-1923].

Hems, Harry. *The Altar and Reredos of Christ Church Cathedral, St. Louis, Mo. With Some Description of the Sculpture Therein Contained, Written Largely in the Words of the Sculptor Himself.* [St. Louis, 191-?].

---. ---. 2nd ed. St. Louis: Eden Publishing House, 1960.

Rehkopf, Charles F. *Christ Church Cathedral, Saint Louis, Missouri: The Cathedral Windows.* [St. Louis?: n.p.], 1972.

Schuyler, Montgomery. *Historical Discourse Delivered at the Semi-Centennial Celebration of Christ Church, St. Louis, 1869.* St. Louis: George Knapp, 1870.

---. *Historical Discourse Delivered on the Occasion of the 70th Anniversary of Christ Church, St. Louis (Now the Cathedral) in the Octave of All Saints' Day, November 3, 1889.* St. Louis: Commercial Printing Company, [1889].

ST. MARK'S

St. Mark's Episcopal Church. *God and Man.* [St. Louis, 1959].

ST. PETER'S

Past and Present of St. Peter's Episcopal Church, St. Louis, Mo. [St. Louis?], 1898.

JUDAISM

B'NAI AMOONA

Bronsen, Rosalind Mael. *B'nai Amoona for All Generations.* St. Louis: Congregation B'nai Amoona, 1982.

TEMPLE ISRAEL

Rosenkranz, Samuel. *A Souvenir Presented at the Golden Jubilee Dinner of Temple Israel, Saturday, October 10, 1936.* [St. Louis, 1936?].

Temple Israel. *70th Anniversary.* [St. Louis, 1956].

UNITED HEBREW CONGREGATION

United Hebrew Congregation. *Dedicatory Book, 1927.* St. Louis, [1927].

LUTHERAN

Baepler, Walter August. *A Century of Grace; A History of the Missouri Synod, 1847-1947.* St. Louis: Concordia Publishing House, 1947.

Graebner, Augustus Lawrence. *Half a Century of Sound Lutheranisn in America: A Brief Sketch of the History of the Missouri Synod.* St. Louis: Concordia, 1893.

Polack, William Gustave. *Fathers and Founders.* St. Louis: Concordia Publishing House, [1938].

Weisheit, Eldon. *The Zeal of His House; Five Generations of Lutheran Church-Missouri Synod History (1847-1972).* St. Louis: Concordia Pub. House, [1973].

HOLY CROSS LUTHERAN

Schneider, Norman H. *Holy Cross Ev. Lutheran Church: Anniversary Issue, 1983.* [St. Louis], 1983.

---. *Holy Cross Lutheran Church: Memorial Issue, 1976.* [St. Louis: Schneider Family, 1976].

IMMANUEL LUTHERAN

Immanuel Lutheran Church. *A Century of Grace, 1847-1947.* [St. Louis, 1947].

---. *Immanuel Ev. Lutheran Church, St. Louis, Missouri: Eightieth Anniversary, 1847-1928.* St. Louis, [1928].

TRINITY LUTHERAN CHURCH

Trinity Lutheran Church. *One Hundredth Anniversary of Old Trinity Lutheran Church, Eighth and Soulard Streets 1839-1939.* St. Louis, [1939].

Rathert, Dennis R. *A History of Trinity Lutheran Church and School.* [N.p..]: Jostens, 1989.

Umbach, Walter O. *Founded Upon Christ: A Brief Historical Summary of Trinity Lutheran Church (The Lutheran Church Missouri-Synod) of St. Louis, Missouri.* [St. Louis], 1966.

METHODIST

History of the United Methodist Churches in Missouri. Ed. Richard A. Seaton. [St. Louis]: Missouri Methodist Historical Society, 1984.

Lewis, W. H. *The History of Methodism in Missouri for a Decade of Years From 1860 to 1870.* Nashville, Tenn.: Pub. House of the M.E. Church, South, 1890.

McAnally, David Rice. *History of Methodism in Missouri From the Date of Its Introduction, in 1806, Down to the Present Day [1840].* St. Louis: Advocate Publishing House, 1881.

Tucker, Frank C. *The Methodist Church in Missouri, 1798-1939; A Brief History.* [Nashville: Parthenon], 1966.

Woodard, W. S. *Annals of Methodism in Missouri: Containing an Outline of the Ministerial Life of More Than One Thousand Preachers and Sketches of More Than Three Hundred: Also Sketches of Charges, Churches and Laymen From the Beginning in 1806 to the Centennial Year, 1884, Containing Seventy-Eight Years of History.* Columbia, Mo.: E. W. Stephens, 1893.

CENTENARY METHODIST
Williams, Francis Emmet. *Centenary Methodist Church of St. Louis, the First Hundred Years, 1839-1939. Compiled for the Centenary Methodist Church in St. Louis, Missouri, in Commemoration of the Inception of its Organization One Hundred Years Ago, and in Honor of the Beginning of Methodism in England Two Hundred Years Ago . . .* St. Louis: Mound City Press, 1939.

The Story of Centenary Church, Saint Louis: Yesterday, Today, Tomorrow. [St. Louis: Shelly Printing Co., 1923].

GRACE CHURCH UNITED METHODIST
Crawford Chapel, Grace Church in the City of Saint Louis, United Methodist. [St. Louis? n.d].

Grace Methodist Church. *Grace Methodist Church: Historical Interpretation, Its Gifts and Memorials.* St. Louis, 1943.

---. *Yearbook of Grace Church -- Holy Cross House, Marion Place, Saint Louis, Mo.* Vol. 4-11. St. Louis, 1914-20.

LAFAYETTE PARK METHODIST CHURCH
Lafayette Park Methodist Church: 115th Anniversary, 1839-1954. [St. Louis? 1954?].
    Includes "A Brief History of Lafayette Park Methodist Church," by Walter A. Godbey.

ST. JOHN'S
Dobler, Mrs. George R., Georgia Gambrill, and Mrs. Adolph Meier. **"St. John's -- An Urban Church Starts its Second Century."** *Missouri Historical Society Bulletin* 25/2 (January 1969): 138-144.

Holt, Ivan Lee. *St. John's Methodist Episcopal Church, South.* St. Louis: Tompkins Prtg. Co., [1938].

St. John's Methodist Church. *The Centennial of St. John's Methodist Church, 1868-1968.* [Compiled by Georgia Gambrill]. [St. Louis, 1968].

St. John's Methodist Church. *Seventy-Fifth Anniversary, St. John's Methodist Church, Kingshighway and Washington, St. Louis: Rev. Albea Godbold, Minister; October 17 to 24, 1943.* [St. Louis], 1943.

UNION METHODIST EPISCOPAL
Union Methodist Episcopal Church. *Dedication and Fifty-Third Anniversary , March 7 to 14, 1913, Union Methodist Episcopal Church, Grand and Delmar Avenues, Saint Louis, Mo.* [St. Louis, 1913?]

PRESBYTERIAN

CARONDELET PRESBYTERIAN
Sims, R. J. **"The Founding of the Carondelet Presbyterian Church."** *Carondelet Historical Society Newsletter* 7/1 (March 1975): 4, 8.

COTE BRILLIANTE PRESBYTERIAN
Graham, Jamie R. *Cote Brilliante Presbyterian Church, 1885-1977.* [St. Louis?]: n.p., 1977.

MARKHAM MEMORIAL PRESBYTERIAN
Markham Memorial Presbyterian Church, St. Louis. Bulletin. Vol. 6-32/33. [St. Louis], 1908-1936.

---. *Installation Service, December 19, 1907, Reverend George W. King, Pastor-Elect.* St. Louis, [1907].

MEMORIAL PRESBYTERIAN
The Memorial Presbyterian Church of Saint Louis: Dedicated December Sixth, Nineteen Hundred Thirty-One. [St. Louis, 1931?].

SECOND PRESBYTERIAN
Bard, Mary G. *A History of Second Presbyterian Church, St. Louis, Missouri, 1838-1977.* St. Louis: Second Presbyterian Church, 1987.

Second Presbyterian Church. *The Fiftieth Anniversary of the Pastorate of Rev. Samuel J. Niccolls, 1865-1915.* St. Louis, [1915].

---. *Handbook and Record.* St. Louis: Bailey, Sage & Co., 1887.

---. *New Century Dinner, 1838-1938, Second Presbyterian Church, Saint Louis, Missouri, Given in Celebration of the One Hundredth Anniversary of the Church, Friday Evening, October Twenty-Eighth, Hotel Jefferson.* [St. Louis, 1938].

UNITARIAN CHURCH

CHURCH OF THE MESSIAH
Church of the Messiah. *Dedication Services of the Church of the Messiah, Dec. 16, 1881.* [St. Louis], 1882.

---. *Church of the Messiah . . . The Order of Services for the Dedication of the New Church, Union Avenue, Corner of Morgan Street, St. Louis, Sunday, December 29th, 1907.* [St. Louis, 1907?].

Swisher, Walter Samuel. *A History of the Church of the Messiah, 1834-1934.* [St. Louis?: n.p., 1934?]

CHURCH OF THE UNITY
Church of the Unity. *Order of Service at the Re-Opening of the Church of the Unity, Sunday, October 11, 1896, Upon the Restoration of the Building After the Tornado of May 27, 1896.* St. Louis, [1896?].

---. *Church of the Unity [Unitarian], Waterman Avenue and Kingshighway, Saint Louis.* [St. Louis, n.d.].

UNITED CHURCH OF CHRIST

CARONDELET UNITED CHURCH OF CHRIST

Carondelet United Church of Christ. *Carondelet United Church of Christ, One Hundredth Anniversary, 1869-1969.* St. Louis, [1969].

FIRST CONGREGATIONAL CHURCH, ST. LOUIS

First Trinitarian Congregational Church and Society of the City of St. Louis. Yearbook. St. Louis, 1900, 1910-11.

Hay, Ellis Walker. *The First Congregational Church of Saint Louis: Centennial, 1852-1952.* [St. Louis?: The Church? 1952?].

PILGRIM CONGREGATIONAL

Pilgrim Congregational Church. *Fiftieth Anniversary of the Founding of Pilgrim Congregational Church, 1866-1916.* St. Louis, 1916.

---. *Pilgrims All!* [St. Louis]: The Church, n.d.

---. *Twenty-Fifth Anniversary, December 5, 6, 7, 8, 1891.* [St. Louis, 1891].

---. *Yearbook.* St. Louis, 1925-52.

Stadler, Frances Hurd. **"Pilgrim Congregational Church: The First Hundred Years..."** *Missouri Historical Society Bulletin* 23/1 (October 1966): 21-51.

Index

Historic Churches & Synagogues
Key to Map

1. **Old Cathedral**
   209 Walnut Street (at Third Street)

2. **St. Mary of Victories Roman Catholic Church**
   St. Stephen's Hungarian Parish
   744 South Third Street (at Gratiot Street)

3. **St. Vincent de Paul Roman Catholic Church**
   1417 S. Ninth Street (at Park Avenue)

4. **SS. Cyril & Methodius Polish National Catholic Church**
   2005 N. Eleventh Street (at Chambers Street)

5. **St. Bridget of Erin Roman Catholic Church**
   1100 N. Jefferson Avenue (at Carr Street)

6. **Christ Church Cathedral**
   320 N. Thirteenth Street (at Locust Street)

7. **St. John the Apostle and Evangelist Roman Catholic Church**
   15 Plaza Square (at N. Sixteenth and Chestnut Streets)

8. **St. Boniface Roman Catholic Church**
   7622 Michigan Avenue (at Schirmer Street)

9. **True Life United Pentecostal Church**
   1426 Warren Street (at Blair Avenue)

10. **Carondelet Markham Memorial Presbyterian Church**
    6120 Michigan Avenue (at Bowen Street)

11. **The Shrine of St. Joseph**
    1220 N. Eleventh Street

12. **Former St. Charles Borromeo Roman Catholic Church**
    2901 Locust Boulevard (at Ewing Avenue)

13. **St. Alphonsus Roman Catholic Church (Rock Church)**
    1118 N. Grand Boulevard (at Cook Avenue)

14. **Holy Cross Lutheran Church**
    2640 Miami Street (at Ohio Avenue)

15. **Centenary United Methodist Church**
    55 Plaza Square (N. Sixteenth Street at Pine Street)

16. **Jamison Memorial Christian Methodist Episcopal Church**
    609 Leffingwell Avenue (at Washington Boulevard)

17. **Carondelet United Church of Christ**
    7423 Michigan Avenue (at Koeln Avenue)

18. **SS. Peter & Paul Roman Catholic Church**
    1919 S. Seventh Boulevard (at Allen Avenue)

19. **Washington Tabernacle Baptist Church**
    3200 Washington Boulevard (at Compton Avenue)

20. **Abyssinian Missionary Baptist Church**
    2126 St. Louis Avenue (at Rauschenbach Avenue)

21. **Memorial Church of God in Christ**
    620 Spring Avenue

22. **Grandel Square Theatre**
    3610 Grandel Square

23. **Scruggs Memorial Christian Methodist Episcopal Church**
    3680 Cook Avenue (at Spring Avenue)

24. **St. Francis Xavier Roman Catholic Church (College Church)**
    3628 Lindell Boulevard (at Grand Boulevard)

25. **St. Agatha Roman Catholic Church**
    3239 S. Ninth Street (at Utah Street)

26. **St. James Community Center**
    1507 E. College Avenue (at Blair Avenue)

27. **Shiloh Church of God**
    4100 Washington Boulevard (at Sarah Avenue)

28. **St. Matthew's United Church of Christ**
    2613 Potomac Street (at Jefferson Avenue)

29. **St. Liborius Roman Catholic Church**
    1835 N. Eighteenth Street

30. **Galilee Baptist Church**
    4300 Delmar Avenue (at Pendleton Avenue)

31. **St. Stanislaus Kostka Roman Catholic Church**
    1415 N. Twentieth Street (at Cass Avenue)

32. **St. Stephen's Lutheran Church**
    515 Pendleton Avenue (at Olive Street)

33. **Berea Presbyterian Church**
    3010 Olive Street (at Cardinal Avenue)

34. **The Church of St. Louis**
    1640 S. Compton Avenue (at Lafayette Avenue)

35. **Cote Brilliante Presbyterian Church**
4687 Labadie Avenue (at Marcus Avenue)

36. **Zion Lutheran Church**
2500 N. Twenty-first Street (at Benton Street)

37. **Centennial Christian Church**
4950 Fountain Avenue (at Aubert Street)

38. **Grace Methodist Church**
340 N. Skinker Boulevard (at Waterman Boulevard)

39. **Most Holy Trinity Roman Catholic Church**
3519 N. Fourteenth Street (at Mallinckrodt Street)

40. **St. John Nepomuk Roman Catholic Church**
1631 S. Eleventh Street (at Lafayette Avenue)

41. **Trinity Lutheran Church**
1805 S. Eighth Street (at Soulard Street)

42. **St. Teresa of Avila Roman Catholic Church**
2413 N. Grand Avenue (at N. Market Street)

43. **Second Presbyterian Church**
4501 Westminster Place (at Taylor Avenue)

44. **Lafayette Park United Methodist Church**
2300 Lafayette Avenue (at Missouri Avenue)

45. **St. John's Methodist Church**
5000 Washington Avenue (at N. Kingshighway Boulevard)

46. **First Church of Christ, Scientist**
477 N. Kingshighway Boulevard (at Westminster Place)

47. **Baptist Church of the Good Shepherd**
500 N. Kingshighway Boulevard (at Washington Boulevard)

48. **Angelic Temple of Deliverance**
5001 Washington Boulevard (at N. Kingshighway Boulevard)

49. **Union Avenue Christian Church**
733 Union Avenue

50. **Pilgrim Congregational United Church of Christ**
826 Union Avenue

51. **Parrish Temple Christian Methodist Episcopal Church**
800 Union Boulevard (at Enright Avenue)

52. **Holy Cross Roman Catholic Church**
8115 Church Road

53. **Immaculate Conception-St. Henry Roman Catholic Church**
3120 Lafayette Avenue (at Longfellow Boulevard)

54. **St. Augustine Roman Catholic Church**
5909 Minerva Avenue (at Hamilton Boulevard)

55. **St. Francis de Sales Roman Catholic Church**
2653 Ohio Street (at Lynch Street)

56. **Cathedral of St. Louis "New Cathedral"**
4431 Lindell Boulevard (at Newstead Avenue)

57. **Pleasant Green Missionary Baptist Church**
4570 Page Boulevard (at Reverend George Pruitt Place)

58. **Pope St. Pius V Roman Catholic Church**
3310 S. Grand Avenue (at Utah Street)

59. **St. Roch's Roman Catholic Church**
6052 Waterman Boulevard (at Rosedale Avenue)

60. **Bostick Temple Church of God in Christ**
5988 Wells Avenue (at Hodiamont Avenue)

61. **St. Ambrose Roman Catholic Church**
5130 Wilson Avenue (at Marconi Avenue)

62. **Memorial Presbyterian Church**
201 S. Skinker Boulevard (at Alexander Drive)

63. **Eighth Church of Christ, Scientist**
6221 Alexander Drive (at Wydown Avenue)

64. **Missouri Historical Society Archives**
225 S. Skinker Boulevard

65. **Immanuel Lutheran Church**
3530 Marcus Avenue (at Lexington Avenue)

66. **Our Lady of Sorrows Roman Catholic Church**
5831 S. Kingshighway Boulevard (at Rhodes Avenue)

67. **St. James the Greater Roman Catholic Church**
1345 Tamm Avenue (at Wade Avenue)

68. **St. Michael the Archangel Russian Orthodox Church**
1901 Ann Avenue

69. **Scruggs Memorial United Methodist Church**
3443 Grace Avenue (at Fairview Avenue)

70. **All Saints' Episcopal Church**
2821 N. Kingshighway Boulevard (at Terry Avenue)

71. **Mount Olive Lutheran Church**
4246 Shaw Boulevard

72. **Mt. Pleasant Missionary Baptist Church**
2854-58 Abner Place (at St. Louis Avenue)

73. **St. Simon Cyrene**
5076 Durant Avenue (at Thekla Street)

74. **St. Nicholas Greek Orthodox Church**
4967 Forest Park Avenue

75. **St. Mark's Episcopal Church**
4714 Clifton Avenue (at Murdoch Avenue)

76. **St. Gabriel the Archangel Roman Catholic Church**
6303 Nottingham Avenue (at Tamm Avenue)

77. **Resurrection Roman Catholic Church**
3900 Meramec Street (at Hydraulic Avenue)